LUCY CALKINS AND LAURIE PESSAH

Nonfiction Writing: Procedures and Reports

DEDICATION

To Tasha Kalista, whose generosity, joy, and dedication have made this project possible.

FirstHand
An imprint of Heinemann
A division of Reed Elsevier Inc.
361 Hanover Street
Portsmouth, NH 03801-3912
www.heinemann.com

Offices and agents throughout the world

TOURO COLLEGE LIBRARY
Kings Hwy

Photography: Peter Cunningham

Rubrics and checklists adapted by permission from *New Standards*. The *New Standards*® assessment system includes performance standards with performance descriptions, student work samples and commentaries, on-demand examinations, and a portfolio system. For more information, contact the National Center on Education and the Economy, 202-783-3668 or www.ncee.org.

Library of Congress Cataloging-in-Publication Data
    Calkins, Lucy McCormick.
    Nonfiction writing : procedures and reports / Lucy Calkins and Laurie Pessah.
    p. cm. — (Units of study for primary writing ; 6)
    ISBN 0-325-00532-X (pbk. : alk. paper)
    1. English language-Composition and exercises-Study and teaching (Primary)--United States. 2. Report writing-Study and teaching (Primary)—United States. 3. Feature writing-Study and teaching (Primary)--United States. 4. Curriculum planning-United States.
    I. Pessah, Laurie. II. Title.
    LB1529.U5C355 2003   2003019535
    372.62'3--dc22

Printed in the United States of America on acid-free paper

07   06   05   ML   4   5

SERIES COMPONENTS

▶ **The Nuts and Bolts of Teaching Writing** provides a comprehensive overview of the processes and structures of the primary writing workshop.

▶ You'll use **The Conferring Handbook** as you work with individual students to identify and address specific writing issues.

▶ The seven **Units of Study**, each covering approximately four weeks of instruction, give you the strategies, lesson plans, and tools you'll need to teach writing to your students in powerful, lasting ways. Presented sequentially, the Units take your children from oral and pictorial story telling, through emergent and into fluent writing.

▶ To support your writing program, the **Resources for Primary Writers CD-ROM** provides video and print resources. You'll find clips of the authors teaching some of the lessons, booklists, supplementary material, **reproducibles** and **overheads**.

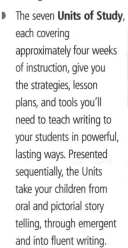

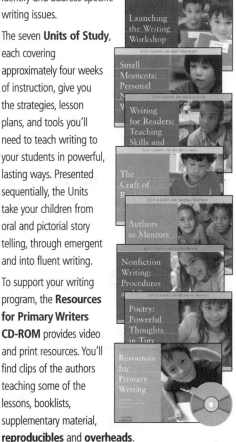

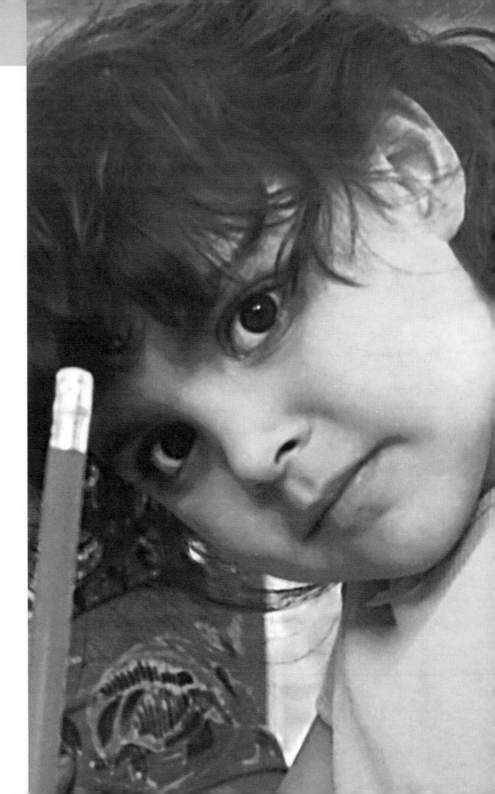

Nonfiction Writing: Procedures and Reports

Every year I read Jane Yolen's *Owl Moon* aloud to children. I love turning the pages of that beautiful picture book, and feeling the silence of that snowy winter evening descend around us. We can almost hear the distant train whistle, "long and low, like a sad, sad song," and the farm dogs that answer back. And when those voices quiet, when it is as quiet as a dream, we can almost hear the crunch of footprints on crisp snow. As we read this book together, we feel what it is to listen for the owl, to listen hard and long, until finally we hear its welcoming call threading through the woods. In *Owl Moon*, it's Pa who takes the child into the woods to search for an owl; but in most of our lives, it is the children who lure us to crunch across the winter snow, to stand under the night sky, to search for an owl, a constellation, a glimpse of the full moon. Children approach the world with wide-eyed curiosity, wanting to listen, to look, to learn.

Years ago, Anna Quindlen wrote this in her New York Times column:

> The lightning bugs are back. They are small right now, babies really, flying low to the ground as the lawn dissolves from green to black in the dusk. There are constellations of them outside the window: on, off, on, off. At first the little boy cannot see them; then suddenly, he does. "Mommy, it's magic," he says.
>
> This is why I had children: because of the lightning bugs. Several years ago I was reading a survey in a women's magazine and I tried to answer the questions: Did you decide to have children: a) because of family pressure; b) because it just seemed like the thing to do; c) because of a general liking for children; d) because of religious mandate; e) none of the above.
>
> I looked for the lightning bugs, for the answer that said, because sometimes in my life I wanted to stand at a window with a child and show him the lightning bugs and have him say, "Mommy, it's magic."[1]

To me, this excerpt says everything about the relationship between children and the world. Because young children are avid students of the world, always ready to peer under a rotting log or to lie on their backs and study the clouds, they respond joyously to an invitation to write about what they know. We tell them, "You'll have to think—what do I know a lot about?" We say, "You could write about Chinese food or laundromats, turning cartwheels, or building Lego castles."

Before we issue the invitation for children to write nonfiction, we need to form a study group with our colleagues in order to mull over, and decide upon, the goals for this unit and the curricular pathways we'll follow.

Why This Unit?

It hardly needs noting that immersing children in nonfiction writing is crucial for them to be able to communicate the truth as they see it about their world. It is crucial too for them to write in these genres in order for them to be able to understand what they read in these genres. From a writer's point of view, they will understand the unique features of the genre, both in terms

---

[1] In *Living Out Loud* by Anna Quindlen (Random House 1988)

of text structures and in terms of authority, perspective, and voice.

Decisions about the writing curriculum in grades K–2 need to be congruent with a school-wide curricular plan, and they need to be made with an eye towards the standards the school has adopted and the standardized tests children will eventually encounter. This is particularly true for non-fiction writing, for this is most apt to be the genre in which children are tested.

Although standardized tests of children's abilities to write usually don't happen until third or fourth grade, writers grow like trees, over months and years, requiring the fullness of time. No crash course or last minute cramming can make writers or trees grow overnight! It's important, therefore, that even primary-grade teachers know what it is children will eventually need to be able to do. The writing we ask children to do in grades K–2 won't exactly mirror the writing they are expected to do eventually, but we do need to be sure that young children develop the writing muscles they will need later, to take the tests and, more importantly, to express themselves and read other's expressions of themselves in the nonfiction genres.

About the Unit

The umbrella of nonfiction writing is a large one: under it fits procedural (or How-To) writing, informational writing (including reports and feature articles and many non-fiction books), and essays and editorials (including literary, historical, and persuasive essays.) Laurie Pessah, a colleague at the Teachers College Reading and Writing Project and it's Deputy Director, and I have found it helpful to divide the terrain for this unit by saying there are three broad categories of nonfiction writing, each requiring different skills:

▸ Procedural (or How-To) writing
▸ Informational writing
▸ Idea-based writing

Procedural Writing

Procedural (or How-To) writing is the most accessible of these. This is especially true for children accustomed to writing tightly sequenced, detailed narratives. To write a How-To book, a child recalls a procedure he or she can do and then lays out the directions for that procedure, starting at the beginning and proceeding in a step-by-step and explicit fashion to the end. Teachers help children write effective procedural texts when we check that their topics and leads *set them up* for the point-of-view, perspective, and sequence required by this genre. If a child wants to write a How-To book on making pancakes and begins the text with, "I love pancakes. Pancakes are great!" a teacher can help by giving the child a new way to start, "Making Pancakes. First you need. . . ."

We can also help children by giving them How-To paper (found in this unit and on the CD-ROM) that has been designed to structure children's writing into a series of steps. The goal when teaching procedural writing will be to help children write with more clarity, sequence, explicit detail, and with the needs of an audience foremost in their minds.

Informational Writing

Informational writing presents new challenges. Many children's first exposure to informational writing comes in third or fourth grade when they are assigned to read difficult non-fiction texts about unfamiliar and conceptually difficult topics such as Ancient Greece. Children are expected to "take notes" (which is something they may never have been taught to do) and then to write a very long report ("in your own words"). Not surprisingly, some children aren't prepared for the barrage of so many new challenges all arriving at once. If we want children to be ready for what they will encounter eventually in school, we need to plan a sequence of opportunities that will equip them by moving them step-by-step along "a gradient of difficulty" in non-narrative writing.

We can support young children's first experiences in writing informational texts by encouraging them to write about subjects in which they already have expertise. It would be vastly easier for you and I to write an informational book on teaching in the primary grades than on Roman aqueducts or the economy of Bali! Eventually, children can write informational books about a whole-class inquiry project (such as seashells), but the place to begin is by inviting children to teach others about a topic around which the child already has expertise and experience.

When children write informational books, we can scaffold this work by explicitly teaching them to divide their topic into sub-topics, each of which becomes a separate chapter. We can further scaffold the work by helping a child see that each sub-topic has an organizational structure. A chapter on "How to Catch a Seagull" is How-To writing and can be written on paper divided into step one, step two, and step three. A chapter on "Kinds of Seagulls" can be written on paper laid out so each kind of seagull is drawn and described in a separate container, perhaps in a separate square. (You'll find these kinds of paper in the unit and on the CD-ROM.) These are some of the ways in which we can provide very strong, explicit scaffolding to help children organize their informational writing.

Idea-Based Writing

By the end of elementary school and the start of middle school, children will be asked to write essays in which they articulate, develop, and defend ideas about topics they've studied. For example, a child may set out to show that a character in a novel "softens up" across the story, or that a character in one book is similar to a character in another book, or that the era known as Westward Expansion was not a time of expansion for the Iroquois.

There are two important ways to help K–2 children develop their muscles so that in time, they can rise to the challenge of this writing. First we need to teach them the skills of accountable talk, and to be sure they learn to use conversation as a forum for having, developing, and defending ideas that are grounded in texts and in information. I detail methods for doing this in *The Art of Teaching Reading*. Second, we need to teach children to write informational texts well. If a child can take a topic like seagulls, divide it into sub-topics, and write with structure, clarity, sequence, and information about those sub-topics, he or she will have the writing muscles necessary to do similar work when the topic is "*Hatchet* and *My Side of the Mountain* are both stories of boys who like to think they can go it alone."

The Course of This Unit of Study

This unit has two parts: first, children write and publish several How-To (or procedural) texts and then they write and publish one large, multi-faceted All About (or informational) book. Teachers needn't follow this plan exactly. Kindergarten teachers might devote the month entirely to writing How-To books. Second-grade teachers might dedicate only one week to How-To writing and reserve more time for children to write an additional All About book on an aspect of the whole class' thematic study topic.

We introduce this genre by telling children they will now become teachers, as well as writers. We ask each child to generate a list of what she can teach others how to do. Then, we model how to write a procedural text. We hold specially designed How-To paper, and, touching each box, we say the step we plan to write in that box. We teach children to test their directions by watching a partner try to follow them. By testing drafts on readers, writers learn how to revise to be more explicit. Children also study published How-To books, noticing some common conventions of the genre: diagrams, numbered steps, and special cautionary comments. Eventually we teach that How-To writing comes in many forms and we expand children's sense of the genre. When children edit their How-To books, we seize this opportunity to teach punctuation especially common in How-To writing: periods, parentheses, and colons.

In the second part of the unit, Children write All-About books.Every unit must have a central message. Here, we want children to learn that sometimes authors write books in order to teach. Erik Erikson, the great developmental psychologist, says, "We are the teaching species. . . . Human beings need to teach not only for the sake of those who need to be taught but for the fulfillment of our identities and because facts are kept alive by being shared, truths by being professed." He is right. When I tell others information I think is valuable, I pause to elaborate on the significance of that information; when I then see the information registering in the learners' minds, I am fulfilling a human need. I am a member of the teaching species. What we sometimes forget is that our children are also part of the teaching species. They, too, need to keep ideas and information alive by teaching them to others. And even five-year-olds have areas of expertise . . . and a human need to teach.

INTRODUCING HOW-TO BOOKS

GETTING READY

- Familiar portion of "Pomp and Circumstance" that you can sing or hum
- Photograph or picture of people graduating, wearing caps and gowns
- How-To book that you have written that can serve as an example (look ahead in the session)
- Chart paper, markers
- Lined paper
- Variety of booklets, each containing about four pages designed to support How-To writing
- Paper for jotting down children's responses that will later be made into a chart
- Ongoing (or new) writing partnerships, each of the partners knowing who is partner one and who is partner two
- Basket of How-To books
- See CD-ROM for resources

INTRODUCE THIS NEW UNIT *by telling your children that they are ready to graduate to a new level. Now they will be* teachers *as well as writers; specifically, they will write to teach others how to do something.*

By sharing the steps in writing a book on how to make cinnamon toast, you'll give your children an overview of the process of writing a How-To book. Then you'll ask the class to retell the steps you took to write a book called How to Make Cinnamon Toast. *In this way, you and the class will co-author* How to Write a How-To Book!

The Minilesson

Connection

Tell your children they're ready to graduate, becoming teachers as well as writers.

"Today is an important day. We start a new unit of study. I have been thinking about the work you have done as writers, and I believe you are ready to graduate to a whole new level. When we finish one level of study, we graduate. We wear hats like this," Laurie held up a photograph of a mortarboard, "and long robes, and we parade in to a song that goes like this." Singing *dee dee-dee-dee dee dee*, Laurie re-created the early section of "Pomp and Circumstance." "Then, we go up on the stage and shake the hand of someone important, who says, 'Congratulations, you are moving on to the next level! It's a higher level. It will be harder, but you are ready for it.' That is what today is all about."

"So pretend you have on these hats and long robes, and . . ." Laurie hummed a bit of "Pomp and Circumstance" with great gusto, then became quiet and spoke into the hush as if she were the graduation speaker. "Congratulations. You are ready to move on to the next level. It will be hard work, but it is important work. Starting today, you will be not just writers—you will also be *teachers*. Very soon each one of you will teach lots of people in this school about something. You will teach by writing *books that teach*."

"Each one of you will write books that teach how to do something."

Remind the children that whenever a writer tackles a new kind of writing, he or she studies examples and gets ready for the new kind of writing.

"Writers, we learned earlier that whenever we want to do a new kind of writing, it helps to study the kind of writing we want to do. Today, we'll study how to write books that teach people to make or do something. I'll teach you how writers go about writing How-To books."

I cherish the wise advice of Jerry Harste,"We need to create, in our classrooms, the kind of world we believe in and then invite our children to role-play their way into being the readers and writers we want them to be." Teaching young children involves equipping them with strategies and skills, but it also involves helping them take on new identities so they each live with a sense of "I am the kind of person who. . . ." In this instance, it is "I am the kind of person who can write books that teach people how to do things."

By the end of Laurie's introduction, her students know what it is that she will teach them, and they know they will learn something they can use not only today but for the rest of their lives.

Teach

Walk children through the steps you took to write a How-To book. Help them list those steps in ways that support their work.

"Last night, I wrote a How-To book like the one you will write today. I'd like you to study the steps I took when I wrote this book. Be ready to list across your fingers the steps I took."

"First," Laurie held onto one of her fingers to remind children they were to make a list across *their* fingers, "I listed possible things I could teach people to do. I could teach you how to. . . ." Laurie turned and read from the list she had written the evening before, her intonation suggesting that this was a list of possible options:

> ### How-To Topics
> ....
> 1. Do a handstand
> 2. Make cinnamon toast
> 3. Play the card game "Go Fish"

"I chose the second thing, how to make cinnamon toast." Laurie held up her first finger and repeated what she'd done. "So I first listed possible topics and selected one."

"Next, I got How-To paper," Laurie held up a formatted paper [*Fig.I-1*], "and planned what I'd write. I did this by sketching one step, the next one, and the next." Laurie pointed to little pictures she'd drawn in each box on her paper.

Before Laurie launches into a detailed discussion, she tells the children how she wants them to listen. She prefaces her example by saying, "Be ready to list across your fingers the steps I took to write this book." This gives children a purpose that directs their attention. The task also sets up the children to think about subjects in a list-the-steps sort of way, which is essential to this unit.

Laurie includes items that are similar to those children might put on their lists. One item involves teaching how to do something, one involves teaching how to make something, and the third, teaching how to play something.

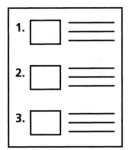

Fig. I-1

Read them your How-To book.

"Then I wrote my book. Listen, you'll see that first I tell the things I need to make cinnamon toast, then I tell the steps in the right order.

> First I get two pieces of toast, some cinnamon, sugar, butter, and a knife.
> Then I butter the bread on one side.
> Then I mix together three spoonfuls of sugar and ten shakes of cinnamon.
> At last I pour that over the bread. If it doesn't stick, I use the knife to push the mixture into the butter.
> Then I eat it!

Active Engagement

Ask children to pretend they are writing a How-To book on writing a How-To book. What would their book say?

"So let's pretend *you're* writing a book on how to write a How-To book. First," Laurie held up one finger, "I listed possible topics (remember?): how to do a handstand, how to make cinnamon toast, how to play cards."

"Keep going. Partner one, tell partner two the next things I did to write a How-To book. List the steps on your fingers."

To give children a running start, Laurie returned to the start of the list and reiterated step 1. "First, I listed possible topics. Then . . . . ?" Laurie held up the special paper as a reminder of the next step.

Children talked in pairs. As they talked, Laurie jotted down what she heard them say so that she could soon say, "I heard you say. . . ."

"Can I stop you? I heard you say:"

How to Write a How-To Book
- First list things you could teach people to do and choose one.
- Then get How-To paper.
- Then plan the steps on the paper.
- Maybe sketch the steps.
- Then write it!
- Write a first page that tells what you need.
- After that, tell the steps in order.

The special paper, like the instructions to list steps across one's fingers, provides concrete scaffolding, helping writers work within the framework of this new genre.

Write and illustrate the simplest piece possible. Make your list the sort of thing you hope your kids will write.

Instead of spending a long time giving children assignments, Laurie gets children started and then passes the baton to them, saying, "keep going."

When a child is reading and gets to a tricky word, it helps to back up and reread. That's essentially what Laurie does now to give her children a running start.

The voice and perspective here is that of a retelling. The children are reciting what Laurie did, not listing the steps a person could take to write a How-To book. Laurie changes the point of view a little in her next statement. How-To books are often written in the imperative (don't tell the children this) to an understood "you." This produces texts which have a distinct tone to them.

"Switch partners. This time, partner two, tell partner one, as clearly as you can, exactly what you would write in a book that taught people how to write How-To books." Holding up one finger, Laurie named step 1. "First, list the things you could teach people to do. Next? Keep going."

After another two minutes of talk, Laurie reconvened the class. "What is the first step in writing a How-To book?" She touched the first box on an empty sheet of How-To paper. A child reported on what he had said to his partner. As he spoke, Laurie recorded his spoken instructions.

"Start again at the beginning and this time, include getting special paper and sketching (or planning the steps on that paper), okay? You can talk across your fingers or touch the boxes on How-To paper as you do this."

Link

Reiterate what the children are saying and, in this way, repeat the directions for this genre.

"I heard you say this." Laurie reread from her notes from earlier. "So writers, let's get started doing these things. Remember that first you must list things you can teach people to do, and choose one thing."

As you send children off, tell them you have a basket full of example texts if they'd like to look at them.

"If you want to look at more examples of How-To books to get an idea of topics, I have a basket of them here."

Laurie sets the voice and tone of procedural writing by getting the children started doing what she hopes they will do. This teaching move happens in both minilessons and conferences. It amounts to teaching by putting someone on a bike and running behind her so she gets going quickly and successfully but without quite realizing what it is she is doing.

Laurie is using the boxes on the paper to help children organize their thoughts. This is especially helpful to her English-language learners. The oral work children are doing serves two purposes: reminding children how to proceed and teaching the tone, language, and structure of the genre. If a child can't speak in this genre, it will be impossible for her to write in it.

When we call on children within a minilesson, we don't simply applaud whatever they say. We coach based on what a child says in hopes that our public coaching of one child rubs off on all the children who observe.

Because Laurie recently read the whole sequence involved in writing a How-To book, the last words she's put into the air have been about the last, not the first, step children are to take. It is a mark of sensitive teaching that she goes back now to reiterate what that first step should be: children list things they could teach others.

Ask children if their topics will allow them to teach someone the steps to take. Show them how to touch each box on the How-To paper and to say what they'd write there.

Laurie spoke over the buzz. "Writers, I know you are either listing topics, or you have started writing. Before you go further, let's check that our topics are good for teaching someone the steps. Remember how before we wrote our small-moment stories, we thought of how the story would go, and we touched each page? Before we write our How-To books, we can touch each box as we say the words we'll write."

Name possible topics and ask children to decide if they lend themselves to How-To writing.

"So I'll say a topic. Pretend it's your topic. Try to touch each box and say the steps. See if it is the kind of topic that has steps."

"The first topic is this: 'The way we play volleyball.' Think in your mind how a book about how to play volleyball would go. (We play it together, so you all should know.) Can you think of the first thing you do to play volleyball?"

"And the next thing you do to play volleyball? If you can think of a next step, thumbs up. Yes? Okay, so 'how to play volleyball' will work as a How-To topic."

"How about 'why my dog is pretty'? Think in your mind if you could teach someone the steps. Can you think of the first thing you would do and the next?"

"No!"

"Smart! But we *could* twist the topic a little. What about this, 'how to make my dog look pretty'? Could you think of a first step you could take? And a second step?"

Across the room, children hoisted their thumbs. "Yes!"

Tell children to share their topics with their partners and imagine how the steps might go.

"Now, will you please turn to your partner and share *your* list of topics? Partners can help each other imagine how the piece might go for each topic. Make sure that for each topic on your list, you can imagine how the steps might go. If one of your topics isn't good for How-To books, cross it off your list. Then you can go back to your writing nooks and continue—or get started—writing."

Don't feel apologetic for asking children to do one kind of writing. Even though these children are five- and six-year-olds and their pieces may be very sweet, you do them no favors if you let them go forward with topics that aren't appropriate for How-To writing.

In order to teach anyone something new, it helps to remind him of what he can already do that is half-way there.

After giving children a second to get started doing this, Laurie joins them in doing it. She holds the How-To paper in her hand, looks at it, and touches the first box as if she is trying to think whether the topic "playing volleyball" could involve steps. She nods to herself.

Again, after a second, Laurie touched the first box, thought "Hmm . . . what could the steps be in a piece called 'Why my dog is pretty?'" Then she carried on, asking children if they could think of steps for that topic.

The topics Laurie suggests are the sort of topics children might write about. This is wonderful active involvement, because children are getting lots of practice at one very specific thing that Laurie wants them each to do.

TIME TO CONFER

At the start of any unit, you always confer toward building enthusiasm for the new work you are beginning:

▶ Set up children so, almost without realizing it, they are saying aloud the exact words that would work splendidly for this sort of writing. Dictate their words back to them, saying, "You've got to write that down!" In this way, you help them get a running start in this new genre.

▶ Help children who seem reluctant or anxious feel a personal connection to the new work. In this instance, you'll help children who say "I have nothing to teach anyone" realize that, in fact, they have topics that the world absolutely needs to learn about.

▶ Create the social network within which children can grow into this new work. This will mean helping partners work well together to generate possible topics and to rehearse for this new kind of writing. See the conference cited at the right from the *Conferring with Primary Writers* book.

▶ Help children understand this genre and get started writing within it. For some children, this means that you will want to help them to learn from published How-To books and to emulate these books without copying them.

Keep in mind that this genre is very accessible. Your proficient writers will take to it like fish to water and probably won't need much support. With some early attention, your inexperienced writers can have a lot of success with this genre—work with them from the start!

Make sure children are addressing topics suited to procedural texts rather than narratives. The mid-workshop advice should help put these writers on track but you could also convene a strategy lesson from the *Conferring with Primary Writers* book.

These conferences in *The Conferring Handbook* may be especially helpful today:

▶ *"What Will You Write in Your Table of Contents?"*

▶ *"If There's No Punctuation, When I Read Your Report It Sounds Like Gobbledygook"*

Also, if you have *Conferring with Primary Writers*, you may want to refer to the following conferences:

▶ "Can I Show You How Writers Find Ideas?"

▶ "What Are You Teaching Your Readers?"

AFTER-THE-WORKSHOP SHARE

Admire the fact that a few children realized they were writing stories, not instructions. Tell about one child, and ask that child to read her work.

"I saw a couple of you stop in the middle of your writing to say, 'Wait—I'm writing a story about what I did one day, not a teaching book.' Brittany had been writing about one time when she went to the beach and made a sand castle, but then she stopped and said, 'Wait a minute! I'm writing a story!'" "Brittany, would you tell everyone about the smart work you are planning to do next? Can you tell us the first step that you will write?"

Brittany pointed to the first box and said, "First you get a flag for the top." Her rising inflection suggested she had no plan to stop with just step1. [*Fig. I-2*]

"Brittany, may I stop you? Let's save the rest as a surprise for another day." Then Laurie returned to the central thrust of the minilesson. "Brittany, can you remind these writers what your topic was at first and why you changed your topic?"

"A*t the start*, I was going to write about one day when I made a sand castle, but it wasn't a How-To, so I changed it to 'How to Make Sand Castles.'"

"It was smart of you to realize that 'One Time at the Beach,' wasn't going to be a teaching book, and it was even smarter for you to switch it around! Congratulations, author." Laurie reached out to shake Brittany's hand.

"Writers, would each of you get with your partner? Partner two, tell partner one the steps you'll write. Partner one, make sure the writer is writing a How-To book."

Brittany is a kindergartner; this is a K–1 class.

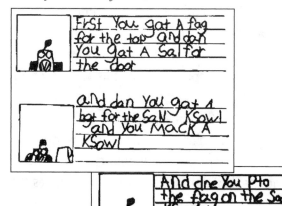

Fig. I-2 Brittany

First you get a flag for the top and then
you get a shell for the door
and then you get a bucket for the sand
castle and you make a castle
and then you put the flag on the sand castle

Don't hesitate to interrupt. The share session is not a prize. Its purpose is not to give a couple of students a few moments in the spotlight but to support all writers. What is happening center stage can only be helpful to everyone if you intervene and steer the talk.

When we teach children, we hope they'll take ownership of new ideas. Brittney has clearly done this. She discusses her shift from one genre to another as if it were totally her own idea. Listening, we delight in her sense of ownership.

IF CHILDREN NEED MORE TIME

Don't be surprised if not all the children have grasped the concepts of this minilesson. You can go forward even if a bunch of your kids still seem to be composing *stories* rather than procedural writing because session II will help them grasp the nature of this genre. But, you may want to linger here for a second day. If you are teaching kindergarteners, for example, you may decide that you want to stretch these first six sessions out into a month-long unit on how-to writing, followed by a month on all-about writing. In that case, you'll probably do a follow-up minilesson after each of the minilessons I describe in detail. If you *do* decide to extend this session, you might:

▶ Show children a published How-To book and say, "Author A wrote this book. I'm pretty sure that, to get started, she first listed things she could teach others about, then she chose to write on this topic. Then she probably got special paper and thought about what the steps would be. She may have sketched them across her pages or touched each step on the paper and said the words she'd write there. Today, I want you to listen to how this author's how-to book goes and get ready to tell your partner three things she has done that you're going to do today in *your* How-To book."

▶ Turn today's mid-workshop teaching point into the minilesson for day two. You can postpone this mid-workshop advice best by delaying the writing. Especially if your children are very inexperienced with this genre, you may want them to spend the first day studying How-To texts and only then list possible topics they could teach others. To make a minilesson out of the mid-workshop advice, you could act out that you are the writer and you are thinking of writing a piece on, say, "My Father's Eightieth Birthday Party." Show the children how you pause, realize your first lead is en route to becoming the story of one time. Adjust the title and genre. Your new piece can be called "How to Give Your Father a Surprise Birthday Party."

Take home your children's work. First check to see if the topics will all support How-To (or procedural) writing. Undoubtedly, some children will be writing pieces that sound more like personal narratives than How-To texts. Catch these kids now before they go further because no amount of crossing out or adding words can turn the one into the other: what's required is a fresh start. A child who has begun writing "The First Time I Got a Home Run" needs you to start him off on a new text titled "How to Hit a Home Run."

You'll also find that some children will have written a different set of (very scanty) directions on each page. For example, Alix titles her book "The How-To Book." Figure I-3 shows the first page of her writing.

Her next page is titled "How to Make a House." [*Fig. I-4*]

Kevin's "How to Rollerblade" runs into the same problem, and although he's older and more skilled, his piece, like Alix's, skims the surface of the steps a learner needs to take. [*Fig. I-5*]

How to make a garden
water
sun
seeds
let it grow
Come back each day

Fig I-3 Alix

How to make a house
I first glue each brick.
Put them together.
Add the roof
and the door.

Fig. I-4 Alix

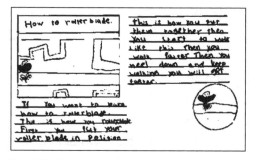

Fig. I-5 Kevin

If you want to learn how to rollerblade
This is how you rollerblade
First you put your rollerblades in position.
This is how you put them together then you start to walk
Like this. Then you walk faster. Then you kneel down and keep walking you will get faster.

CHECKING FOR CLARITY

GETTING READY

- Sample book from the previous session: *How to Write a How-To Book*
- See CD-ROM for resources

IN THE PREVIOUS SESSION, YOU INVITED YOUR CHILDREN *to write books that teach people how to do things. You showed them a book you'd written and said, "List topics on which you could teach." Then, after they had each chosen a topic as a starting place, you urged them to articulate, then sketch, and finally write the steps involved in the activity they wanted to teach someone to do. You begin this session knowing that some of your children got off to a good start and that others need to revisit the sort of thing you want them to write. This means that this minilesson needs to be especially multilevel. For some children, the point will be to give them another big picture of what it means to write How-To books. For other children, you hope to help them take their initial work further.*

Your plan is to help all the children understand the purpose and requirements of this genre by showing them that How-To writing must enable a reader to do the activity that is being taught. A writer of directions needs, above all, to give readers the clear, step-by-step instructions necessary so the reader manages to do the job. Writing so that readers learn to do something is the essential characteristic of this genre, and you'll convey this fact today.

THE MINILESSON

Connection

Report with enthusiasm on the How-To writing that children initiated earlier.

"Most of you have gotten started planning How-To books that teach kids to do something. Sam will teach us how to do a somersault, Serena will teach us how to catch a Frisbee, and Jorge will teach us how to get a dog at the SPCA. It's going to be great to learn all these things!"

Tell children there is one more step in How-To writing: writers read the directions to a learner and watch the learner attempt to follow the directions.

"There is another step I need to add to our book on how to write How-To books: whenever you write How-To books, after you get started, you need to check whether your directions will work. Today I'll teach you one way to do that."

Teach

Suggest that the best way to check whether the directions work is to read them to a friend who tries to follow them.

"The best way to check whether your directions work is to read them to a partner who will try to do the thing you are teaching (for real or for pretend). Then, if your directions don't *quite* work, you can revise them. So I need to add another step to our book!"

HOW TO WRITE A HOW-TO BOOK
....

First list things you could teach people to do and choose one.

Then get How-To paper.

Then plan the steps on the paper.

Maybe sketch the steps.

Then write it!

Write a first page that tells you what you need.

After you write, recheck your directions with a partner.

We teach children that good writing is detailed, and the same is true of a good minilesson. These examples provide children with details they can emulate. By citing what some writers have done, I convey the message, "This is the sort of work we should all be doing." This allows the minilesson to reinforce the earlier message. By saying I can't wait to learn what these writers will teach, I highlight the fact that my goal for children is that they write in ways that are instructive.

A couple of lessons can be learned here. First, this minilesson dovetails with and builds on the previous one. It will be far easier for children to remember both minilessons because they build on the same overall injunction. Then, too, I preface my comments with phrases such as "Whenever you write How-To books," which remind children that this minilesson is not meant simply to assign them work for today but instead is meant to inform them about something they can do whenever they write within this genre.

Laurie has turned her notes from the previous session into a chart to which you can add.

Use a child to help you demonstrate what it means to check your directions with a partner.

"I'll show you what I mean by checking that your directions work. Sam is writing a book on doing a somersault. I'm going to be his partner." I brought Sam to sit on a chair beside my chair. "Sam will read me his book (just the start—it isn't done), and I'll do whatever his book tells me to do. Guys, when you do this kind of reading—when you read directions—instead of reading it straight through, it helps to read one step and then do it, then read the next step, then do it."

Sam, sitting in the chair beside me, read, "First put your head down and your legs up." Still sitting on a chair at the front of the meeting area, I tucked my chin toward my chest and sagged my head (remember I was still on the chair!). "Okay, I put my head down . . . hmm . . . my legs up?" I raised my feet so they stuck straight out from the chair. "Keep reading."

Sam had covered his eyes in dismay. "Then turn over?" Everyone laughed. "Turn over? I'll hurt myself!"

Sam started to protest that when he told me to put my head down, he meant I needed to put my head on the floor and that of course I needed to get off the chair to do so, but I returned to the role of teacher rather than gymnast-to-be. "Are you saying, Sam, that now you realize you need to make revisions to your directions? That's what happens when you do this step." I tapped on the final item I'd added at the end of the chart:

> After you write, recheck your directions with a partner.

Active Engagement

Ask children to think with their partners about ways to revise the original instructions. Collect their suggestions, then try following the revised instructions.

"Would you tell your partner how you might start a book on doing somersaults that could maybe work better?"

"Okay, let's try out another set of directions for doing a somersault. Just tell me your new sense of the steps, and I'll follow them."

"Sit on the floor."

I looked over the children's books ahead of time and selected one that would make the point I wanted to make. I also made sure the writer had a robust enough self-concept and would be game for me to use his or her piece in this fashion.

Have some fun while you teach, and let the kids have some fun, too.

One of the characteristics of a good minilesson is cohesion. The parts fit together. It's important that I cycle back to this chart several times in this minilesson.

First I help the whole class do something, and then I recruit every student to do the same thing more independently. One can almost see the baton being passed, and the transition is as smooth as in a good relay race.

I knew from the start that I wouldn't actually flip around in the air in front of my class! But my kids are enthralled at the prospect, and I'll help them see that their improved directions get me off to a better start than when I tried a somersault from the chair.

"Okay, first you sit on the floor." I added the phrase *first* to the child's text as I clamored off the chair. "Okay, I've done that. What's next?"

"Put your head on the floor."

I touched my face to the floor, not putting my head in the proper position.

"No! Put the *top* of your head. . . ."

"That's a smart revision! Put *the top of your head* on the floor. You are getting better at realizing the details your readers will need. I don't think I want to do the next steps right now, so let's stop, but that was good work, writers. You are thinking about your reader and trying to say the steps in a way that will work for your reader."

Link

Send children off to read their directions to a partner, who will then try to follow those directions. Children give feedback to writers, who then revise their original directions.

"Today, instead of going back to our places, will you and your partner find a bit of floor space? We're going to start by reading the directions we've already written to our partners. Partner one, read one step, then let your partner do it, then read the next step and let your partner do it. We won't have all the equipment here in this room to actually follow the steps. That'll happen often with How-To writing, so you have to pretend to do the steps. Pretend to be scrambling the eggs or painting the fence—but as you do it, think, 'Would I do the right thing if I follow the directions the writer is giving?' After you've learned what works and what doesn't work in your directions, you can rewrite them—and then keep going."

"Get started in your partnerships. In five minutes, we'll all start writing and rewriting."

In this genre, the writer often writes directly to his or her reader. The writer says, "You need to . . . then you should." In every other genre it is preferable to write with the pronouns I or she/he, not you. This genre is an exception.

When you want to praise what a writer has done, rename the thing so that it can be transferred to another text and another day. If you said, "You added that I must put the top of my head on the floor . . . that's smart," this compliment wouldn't easily translate into an injunction influencing future actions. But by naming the wise action in a generic way—"You thought about your reader and tried to say your steps in a way that will work for your reader"—you help children extrapolate lessons from today that can pertain to tomorrow.

If you worry that this will be an invitation to chaos, you can settle for asking writers to read directions to themselves and imagine what their readers will make of each step. But I recommend letting other kids try out the directions.

TIME TO CONFER

Use your conferences and strategy lessons to be sure every child is engaged with the central thrust of this unit. Your upcoming minilessons will only work if children have a How-To book underway.

Previously you will have noticed that a few children hadn't yet gotten started writing How-To books. Watch these children's productivity at the start of the writing workshop today, and if it seems that they plan to wait idly until you give them each a personal jump-start, consider convening a strategy lesson; the conference "Partners Can Help Each Other Come Up With Ideas" will help you.

You will no doubt find that when some children reread their rough drafts of How-To books to each other and tried to actually follow each other's directions, they learned their drafts were problematic. It's one thing to know there's a problem and another to have strategies for fixing the problem. See the conferences cited at right.

You will encounter children who will tell you they can't follow each other's directions. "I can't ski in this room, can I?" they'll say. You need to show children that they can read each other's directions and imagine following them, and that doing this can chase out potential problems in the directions. See "Monitoring for Sense."

This conference in *The Conferring Handbook* may be especially helpful today:

▶ *"Make a Mental Movie of Yourself Following Your Directions to Test Them for Clarity"*

Also, if you have *Conferring with Primary Writers*, you may want to refer to the following conference:

▶ "Which Part Goes Where?"

Ask children to join you in listening and mentally following one child's directions.

"Today, I saw many of you reading directions not only to your partner but also to yourselves. You reread what you wrote and thought 'If I follow my own directions, will they work?' I have asked Nicole to read her How-To book to us. As she reads, let's close our eyes and see if we can picture ourselves doing each of these steps."

Nicole read her writing. [*Fig. II-1*]

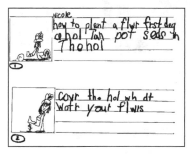

How to Plant a Flower
First dig a hole.
Then put the seeds in the hole.

Cover the hole with dirt. Water your flowers.

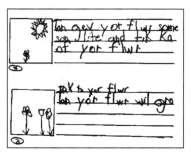

Then give your flower some sun light and take care of your flower.

Talk to your flower. Then your flower will grow.

Fig. II-1 Nicole

Nicole hadn't yet finished the book, but she told her classmates what she planned to write on the final page: "One day it will start to grow."

"Thumbs up if you were able to see the steps of that happening." Thumbs went up across the room. "I feel ready to plant a flower right now!"

Send the children off to read aloud to their partners, who will listen, trying to imagine doing the steps.

"Writers, would you get with your partners? Partner two, read your book to partner one, just like Nicole read her book to us. And partner one, listen and see if you can picture yourself doing each step. Are the directions clear? Do you know what to do first and next and next?"

When one child reads or speaks within a whole-class meeting, our role is to model what it means to be an attentive listener. This requires not only that we be such listeners but that our body language convey to the large group of listeners the message "Come on, now, let's you and I really listen." We need to be in solidarity with the class, listening together to the child who speaks or reads.

If you really attend to the text, there is at least one confusing thing. The directions suggest that we must cover the seed with dirt. Then it says, "Give your flower some sunlight." Reading this, we envision that a flower has emerged. But the book ends, "One day it will start to grow," as if the seed hasn't yet sprouted. Be attuned to this sort of inconsistency, but chances are you'll keep it to yourself!

I listened in as Troyquon turned to his partner, Rita, and began to read: [*Fig II-2*]

Rita interrupted at this point. "How will it look like a pizza, not a donut?"

I agreed. "Rita is asking a good question. That's so helpful, isn't it Troyquon? With that help, you can go back and reread and think, 'Have I told her enough?'"

Troyquon looked dubious about reconsidering his text, and it was time for the share session to end. Seizing the moment, I said, "I'll tell you what—why don't I take your directions home and try following them. I'd love to eat some pizza tonight!"

Troyquon took a sticky note and carefully wrote his telephone number. "If you need me, call me."

I told the class that I knew they all wanted to plant a flower after hearing Nicole's writing and that I now had dinner plans!

Fig II-2 Troyquon

A Cook Book
How to Make Pizza
Throw up the dough.
Spin the dough in your fingers.
Put the dough into a flat circle.
Put tomatoes onto the dough.
Put cheese on the dough.
Put the dough into the pan.

Notice that I speak of suggestions (or, we could say, criticisms) as help: it's wise for us to act as though we've been given great gifts when someone points us toward revisions, even though the truth is that most of us sympathize with anyone who resists revision!

It is crucial that you find a child who has written a recipe and offer to take it home and do some cooking. It is also crucial for you to get the child's phone number! Look ahead to Session III. This plays a critical role in that session.

If you have time, ask the partners to switch so each child gets a chance to read aloud, but if time is short, this is not essential. Both partners learn even if only one partner's writing is reread and reconsidered—and there is always tomorrow.

When teaching writing, the problems children encounter are not cause for despair. Instead, the problems are crucial because they give us our direction. Study the source of problems so that your next minilessons and strategy lessons address the issues.

If your children are choosing topics that don't set them up to write procedural pieces, spend more time immersing children in the sounds of procedural writing. Read How-To writing aloud. Don't talk this reading to death. Just read and immerse your children in the sounds of the genre. Meanwhile, find opportunities to give the class oral directions. "Today we're going to make butterflies. Let me teach you how. Listen. I'm going to give you all the How-to directions now. First you. . . ." Meanwhile, help children develop lists of topics that match the genre, and key phrases as well: Do you want to know how to . . . ? I will teach you. First you. . . .

If your children are taking giant steps through the process they are trying to teach, assuming that their reader will understand more than the reader could possibly understand, have children continue reading their directions aloud step by step to a partner, who either follows the directions by performing each step or pretends to do this. It will be important for these readers to say "I'm confused" when they feel confused. You could lead a minilesson or a strategy lesson in which you say, "I found this book, How to Make Peanut-Butter-and-Jelly Sandwiches, on my desk this morning [you're pretending—you wrote it] and thought we'd try out the directions. Sammy, would you read it aloud?" So Sammy reads, "Get jelly, peanut butter, and bread." You put a pretend jar of jelly, peanut butter, and a loaf of bread in front of you and look up for the next step. "Put the jelly on the bread." You stand the jar of jelly on the loaf of bread. Children will find this very funny, and meanwhile they will learn.

There is a rhythm to the assessments you do while teaching writing. At the start of a unit, you have your hands full getting everyone on board, and therefore you don't have a chance to observe the class at work. During these early days, however, you will be keen to see how many of your children are well launched and intent on identifying kids who need support so you can give them the direction or assistance they need. This means that after Session I and/or II in any unit of study, you will definitely collect your children's work and take it home to examine. The folders for the new unit will still be thin (and you don't have to beat yourself up if the kids are having difficulties). The questions to ask are clear: "Who is well launched? Who is in trouble? What are the biggest sources of difficulty?"

The next phase of assessment comes a day or two later, when you feel the unit is past the starting block. Now you can stop rescuing kids and can begin to observe the patterns in the room. You should be able to take five minutes during the writing workshop to observe your kids working with the new genre. The workshop will be different because children are writing procedural pieces. Children will be drawing again, but this time the drawings will serve the reader as much as the writer. Some children will churn these books out at a terrific clip. Their writing may take on an informal, oral tone such as you see in Jen's text. [*Fig. II-3*]

Finally, you'll probably discover that a few writers who haven't been particularly adept will shine in this genre. Help this happen. If these children get off to a strong start with nonfiction writing, and if you then use their work as examples for others to emulate, you can build their confidence.

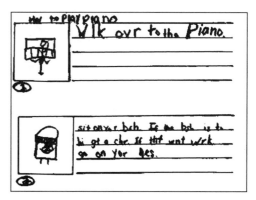

Fig. II-3 Jen

How to Play Piano
Walk over to the piano.
Sit on your bench. If the bench is too high get a chair.
If that won't work, go on your knees.

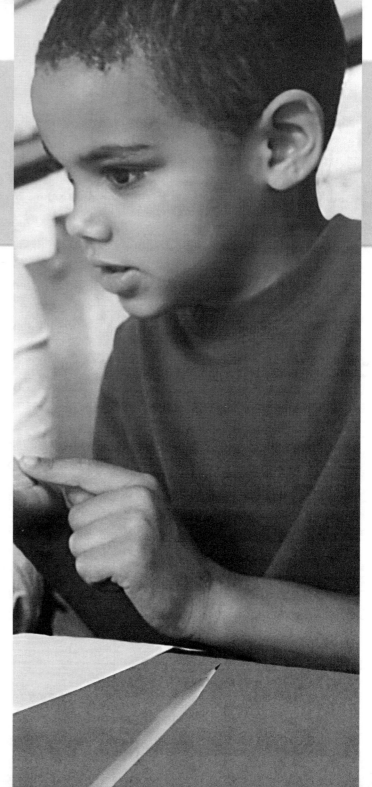

REVISING WORDS AND PICTURES

GETTING READY

- Child's How-To draft that is confusing to follow
- Sticky notes
- Whiteboards
- See CD-ROM for resources

A FAMOUS WRITER ONCE SAID, *"Poetry is the school I went to in order to learn to write prose."* *Every genre of writing has lessons to teach young writers. From studying How-To writing, children can learn to write explicit, clear, sequenced texts—and they can learn to reread their own drafts anticipating the confusion readers will encounter. These lessons are of fundamental importance. They aren't easy lessons because young children don't have an easy time assuming someone else's point of view. It's not a small accomplishment for a five-year-old to imagine that his or her reader won't necessarily have the knowledge required to be able to follow the child's intended meaning.*

You won't want to miss the chance to teach children to reread their own and one another's directions, asking "Is this clear?" in ways that reveal gaps and confusions. In this lesson, you'll show children how you tried to read one child's directions and encountered confusions. You'll also show how the author can revise his words and his pictures to be sure they are more detailed and explicit.

The Minilesson

Connection

Tell your children that writers often leave out steps. Our first drafts aren't always clear. Today children will learn how to find and revise their own confusing parts.

"Writers, last time you read your books aloud to each other and those of us who were listening tried to follow your directions in our minds. Sometimes we said to the writer, 'Wait, I'm a bit confused.' That almost always happens when we write How-To books. We leave out steps, or we don't write everything clearly. Today I'll show you how writers read our own How-To books, hoping to find the confusing parts. I'll show you how we revise to fix those parts."

Teach

Tell the children you took one child's writing home and that your friend read it aloud while you tried to follow the steps. Solicit a volunteer to read the text aloud and reenact the confusion you ran into.

"Troyquon read his book, *How to Make Pizza*, to Rita yesterday, and Rita was a little confused. So I offered to take Troyquon's book home and try making pizza. Let me tell you what happened."

"I cleared off the kitchen counter so I was ready, and I asked my husband to read me the directions. Amos, will you pretend to be my husband and read me the steps?" Laurie passed the book over to Amos, who read, "Throw up the dough." Laurie, pretending she was sitting at the kitchen counter ready to cook pizza, said, "What?" and gestured to show that she wasn't one bit sure how to throw up the absent dough. "Read that again, because I'm confused."

"Throw up the dough."

"What dough?"

Tell the children that when you encountered a confusing part in the directions, you phoned the author, who clarified the directions for you so you could continue.

Slipping out of her role for an instant, Laurie said to the class, "The good thing is that Troyquon gave me his phone number, so I called and he said, 'First

When we teach people to do something—to swim or to teach or to write procedural texts—one of the difficulties is that we need to decide what matters. What skills do we want to be sure learners develop? It'd be easy to teach writers details about the features one finds in How-To texts. The trick is to steer our teaching away from Trivial Pursuits! Here, Laurie and I have decided that we really want children to grasp the idea that How-To books are written for readers who read sequenced, clear directions.

Whenever you are dramatizing in front of children, the trick is to really focus on the action you are recreating. Your mind needs to be on the cooking endeavor and not on the fact that you are performing for the class. Can you picture your counter at home? Pull your chair closer in to it. You should be able to feel the counter's edge, to run your hands along the imaginary counter. Give it substance (in your mind's eye). Now, listen to the directions as if you are only now hearing them for the first time. "Throw up the dough." Your reaction—"Huh? What dough?"—should feel organic and real if you are really focused and lost in the moment.

buy a bag of pizza dough and then take the dough out of the bag.' I had some in my refrigerator, so I followed his directions. I could start over." Laurie settled back into role playing. "Read again what I do."

"Throw up the dough."

Laurie looked at the imaginary dough in her hands. She looked back at Amos. "You're serious?"

The class, anticipating what was about to happen, laughed. "So I did it." Laurie took the imaginary dough and heaved it toward the ceiling. It descended; she caught it and threw it spiraling high into the air again. Then she turned to Troyquon, "Making pizza sure is fun! Am I doing it right?"

Continue to reenact how you followed the directions incorrectly; this time, let the author step in to rescue you.

Troyquon said, "No, you do it like this," and took his turn with the imaginary dough.

"Oh! I get it."

Signal that the drama is over. Tell children that your point is that writers of How-To books need to find and fix confusing sections in their texts.

Laurie signaled that both Amos and Troyquon could sit down, and she waited for the class to give her their serious attention.

"Writers, whenever we write How-To books, we need to try hard to read them in such a way that we find the confusing parts, as Troyquon and I have now done. Let me show you what Troyquon did next—it's smart work."

Show children that some writers used sticky notes to mark confusing parts as a way to guide future revision.

Laurie held up Troyquon's draft to show that he had added a sticky note on page one. She read what he had written, "Tell where you got it," to remind himself to explain the origin of the dough. He had put another sticky note beside his instructions to "throw up the dough." On this one, he'd written, "Tell how."

Pause before and after you ask "You're serious?" Then maybe recruit your "husband" to reread the directions yet again. You want every child in the room to listen to those directions and to be in your shoes, thinking along with you that they can't believe you are really supposed to throw the dough into the air.

A major secret to good management is that we need to wait until children have given us their attention before we continue talking. Don't talk over your children. Wait until they are with you.

Active Engagement

Recruit the class to help the author clarify a confusing section of his How-To book.

"Writers, sometimes confusing sections are easy to fix. Troyquon, am I right that it will be easy to add a sentence about buying the dough?" Troyquon nodded. "But writers, sometimes we come to parts that aren't very easy to explain. Troyquon, am I right that it will be tricky to explain how to throw the pizza dough?" Again Troyquon nodded. "Troyquon, will you pretend to do it, and we'll all try to figure out how to put that on the paper? Let's all try to find the words to explain this tricky part."

Troyquon stood up and reenacted the way he throws up pizza dough.

Ask children to tell their partner how they'd explain a confusing action.

"Partner one, tell partner two what you'd say. Troyquon, do it one more time." Troyquon made the motion, and the room buzzed.

Call children back together. Tell them that sometimes writers make pictures to help explain how to do something.

"Writers, may I stop you? I heard you working hard to find the words to make this clear. It isn't easy, is it? I want to tell you one more hint. Often, writers use teaching pictures to explain how to do something. Let's see if we can draw a picture of what Troyquon means by throwing up a pizza, okay? Partner one, bring out your whiteboard and divide it in two.

"Troyquon, would you throw up the pizza one more time, and then partner one, will you draw the first thing he does? Then partner two, you draw the next thing. The drawings should explain how to do it."

Link

Tell children that they can mark their confusing parts with sticky notes and then revise.

"Writers, whenever you write How-To books, you need to pretend you are the reader and read your own writing, thinking, 'What's confusing?' Then revise those parts to make sure your teaching is clear."

If you want to give children practice rereading their texts (and one another's) to find confusing sections, you could now read another student's How-To book aloud and have each child mentally (or through small actions that he or she can do while sitting on the rug) follow the directions enough to spot confusions and tell them to his or her partner.

Because these children have already been doing this work with their partners, Laurie instead decided to move on to make a second teaching point. The architecture of minilessons shouldn't be a straightjacket, it's fine to decide to structure some minilessons differently.

TIME TO CONFER

Now that the unit is well launched and you've taken the time to read the room and to address the biggest issues you saw, you may want to reflect on your own progress as a teacher of writing. Think especially about your progress in learning to confer.

Most teachers I know go through a phase when they are worried what to say in conferences. Carl Anderson, author of *How's It Going*, a book on conferring, tells of a time when he brought cue cards into his conferences with questions to ask:

- What are you working on as a writer?
- How's it going?
- What are you planning to do next?
- What might you do if you were going to revise?
- Could you show me that?

For most of us, the breakthrough comes when we lose some of that early self-consciousness by really and truly focusing on the child. Real listening is vastly more difficult than you might think. When I was a kid, learning to play tennis, my mother used to call out, "Keep your eye on the ball" and I'd think "What do you think I'm doing, watching birds? *Of course* I'm keeping my eye on the ball." But since then, I realized that really, truly watching the ball, like really, truly listening in a conference, is extraordinarily difficult.

Try it. Go into the workshop intending to really listen. Try above all to understand what the child is trying to do and why she's trying to do that, and try to understand how this work fits into the larger story of this child as a writer and a person. Plan to be entertained, amazed, informed, and moved by the spirit that's there, inside each and every writer.

These conferences in *The Conferring Handbook* may be especially helpful today:

- *"Make a Mental Movie of Yourself Following Your Directions to Test Them for Clarity"*
- *"What Will You Write in Your Table of Contents?"*
- *"If There's No Punctuation, When I Read Your Report It Sounds Like Gobbledygook"*

Also, if you have *Conferring with Primary Writers*, you may want to refer to the conferences in part six.

Explain to the children that they need to spell carefully to be understood.

"Writers, today *you* read your directions aloud to your reader. In real life, *you* won't always be there with your book, able to read it aloud. You need to write so that *readers* can read your writing. And if readers are trying to learn what to do next, they can't take ten minutes to figure out what your words say. If you told someone how to make pancakes, and he put the batter in the frying pan but then it took ten minutes to read, "Flip the pancakes," by the time he got to flipping them, the pancakes would be burnt! So you really need to try to spell correctly so that readers can read your writing."

Using an example from the class, ask children to practice spelling a difficult word with their partners. Ask the original writer if he'd like to revise his spelling after the class has helped.

"Roger is writing about how to hatch chick eggs. His directions begin [*Fig. III-1*], 'First you need a *fertilized egg*. A rooster makes it fertilized.' Would you and your partner see if you can help him spell *fertilized*?

"Remember, break it into chunks. Say a chunk, then think, 'Do I know any words that have this chunk, this sound?' Use the words you know to help you spell even brand new words like *fertilized*. Go to it.

"Can some of you put your best guesses on the board, and we'll see if Roger might decide to change his first spelling?" They did, and Roger changed *pherdaliysd* to *pherdaliysed*.

Ask children to apply this spelling work to a classmate's writing.

"Writers, will each of you share your How-To book with a reader who has never read it before? Let the reader read it. You should notice places where the reader has a hard time reading. See if you can work together to change what you've written so your next reader doesn't run into the same trouble."

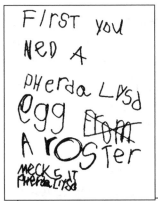

First you need a fertilized egg a rooster makes it fertilized

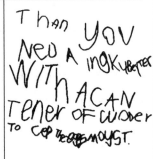

Then you need an incubator with a container of water to keep the eggs moist.

Fig. III-1   Roger

By now, in the light of what you know about your children's work with How-To writing, you'll want to give some thought to your overall plan for this unit. We've designed the unit in two halves. We imagine you'll spend just less than two weeks teaching your children How-To writing and that you'll then switch and teach them informational (or All-About) writing.

However, you may instead decide to spend a full month on How-To writing, followed by a full month on informational writing. How-To writing is a very accessible genre. It's action oriented and interactive, and it may help children develop a feeling of expertise and authority. These qualities make the genre especially good for English-language learners.

On the other hand, if children spend a long time writing How-To books, they become accustomed to writing in a voice and point of view that is closer to oral language than to literary language. Like writing with ellipses or exclamation points, the tone and point of view of How-To writing can take root quickly and overwhelm other ways of writing.

Our point is only that before you progress further in this unit, you'll want a game plan. If you plan to make this into a month-long study, you'll pace yourself differently starting now.

Meanwhile, you'll want to use the rubric and conferring guides to help you notice what your children have (and have not) learned thus far in this unit. Decide on what you think are the aspects of How-To writing that you will want to highlight in your teaching.

INCORPORATING FEATURES OF HOW-TO WRITING

GETTING READY

▶ Transparency of a How-To page from Gail Gibbons' *The Pumpkin Book*
▶ Overhead projector
▶ Chart, markers
▶ Basket of How-To books
▶ Smaller version, in the form of a checklist, of the class chart "How-To Helpers" for each child
● See CD-ROM for resources

ALL OF YOUR CHILDREN WILL HAVE FINISHED *a draft of at least one and probably several How-To books. Now is a good time to help them raise the level of the books they've completed and of the books they have yet to write. One way to do this is to encourage your youngsters to notice special features of this genre and to incorporate these features into their writing.*

Today, as you turn your children's attention to the features of How-To writing, you may want to help them understand that the features aren't rules. They exist only because writers want to use every means possible to teach readers. If we give an oral presentation, we refer to our transparencies not only because that's what speakers often do, but also because this helps our listeners organize and remember what we are saying. Similarly, the features of a How-To book help readers comprehend and follow the directions. Today, you'll teach your children that as writers of How-To books, they probably want to give their readers "helpers," as you'll call the text features of this genre.

THE MINILESSON

Connection

Remind the children that they already know they can use exclamation points and ellipses to help people read their writing well.

"Writers, you know that when you write, there are things you can do to tell people how to read your writing. You can add exclamations marks—!—to signal to readers, 'Read this like it is exciting!' and you can add ellipses to help readers know they need to slow their voices down."

Referring to a sentence I'd written on chart paper, I said, "For example, in this sentence I use ellipses to tell my readers to slow their voices down when they read this sentence: 'I took one step . . . then another step . . . then another step.'"

Tell the children that today they are going to learn ways writers help readers follow directions.

"Today I want to tell you that when we write How-To books, there are little things we can do to help readers read *and follow* our directions."

Teach

Use an overhead projector to show the features of How-To writing that one author used.

"Let's look at a How-To page from Gail Gibbons' *The Pumpkin Book*. I'm going to read it aloud and show you what I mean about writers doing things to help readers out. Then I'll give you each another How-To book to investigate, and together we'll check whether authors of other How-To texts do similar things."

"I'll point out what I see in this book. Then you can investigate whether the same features are present in other books." Using an overhead projector, I displayed the selected page on the wall.

During the connection component of a minilesson we often reiterate the previous minilesson before teaching children the new focus of today's work. Because today's minilesson builds more on prior work with the conventions of writing than on prior work with How-To writing, I help the children remember that they've already had great success learning about conventions of writing. I want to convey that today's minilesson continues on a trajectory of success. I also want to put them in a mindset to understand the kind of thing I refer to when I speak about text features.

We teach the features of How-To writing by emphasizing that these features matter because they offer readers helpful assistance.

To set my learners up so they'll listen well, I tell them why I'm going to read this page from The Pumpkin Book. *I even tell them explicitly what I hope they will notice. I could elicit what they notice on the page I've selected, but I needn't feel embarrassed about plain-out teaching what I want them to see. There are lots of other opportunities to elicit children's observations. One such opportunity comes during the active engagement phase of this minilesson.*

List features you notice across your fingers. Start by noticing that the writer has titled the book how to do something. This title sets up expectations for the reader.

"The first thing I notice," I held up a finger to signify I was making a list, "is that Gail Gibbons gives me a helper because she names her page '*How to Carve a Pumpkin.*' As a reader, I now know this will be How-To writing, and I'm ready to read it in a step-by-step way. I am ready to read one step and then do it (or imagine doing it), then read the next step. So the first helper is, *she titles her writing* in ways that help readers predict."

Continue reading the example. Using your next two fingers, list additional features you notice: how she begins with needed materials and how she uses pictures.

"So let's read on, and I will continue to point out ways that Gail Gibbons helps her reader. The page starts like this:"

How to Carve a Pumpkin
1. ALWAYS have an adult help you.
2. Take a knife that is not too sharp or a special cutter used
for carving pumpkins and cut the lid off the pumpkin.

Touching my second finger, I said, "So now I see that the next way Gail helps readers is that she tells what things I will need before I can start carving a pumpkin."

Then, touching my third finger, I said, "And I'm noticing that the pictures aren't regular pictures. They don't show the place where the pumpkin is—the trees and the sky. The picture just shows what the words say. The picture teaches readers what to do—the third helper I see."

Show children a chart on which you list the features that you have just identified and use it to recall what you found.

"So in this book, the author gives readers these helpers." I showed them the list on chart paper:

I refer to the features of this genre as "helpers." You'll need to decide whether you want to use the term helpers *instead of* text features. *Perhaps you prefer the formal term. I am ambivalent about creating a whole new metalanguage, and yet when the kids take to terms like this with such obvious relish, my ambivalence disappears.*

I am succinct. I have a lot of ground to cover and need to speak succinctly.

Each feature I listed could be the subject of an entire minilesson or strategy lesson. For example, I could teach a minilesson highlighting the differences between most illustrations and the diagrams. Discussing all these items in combination in this minilesson doesn't preclude me from teaching more minilessons about each of these points. It is not unusual to first do a minilesson that lays out the broad terrain and then follow up with another minilesson or two that explore specifics more deeply.

HOW-TO HELPERS
....

1. A title that says this will be a How-To book
2. A list of the things we'll need
3. Pictures that teach us what to do

Active Engagement

Pass out How-To books for the children to study; ask them to look for similar or different features.

"I'm going to pass out some other How-To books. Would you and your partner look at these books and see if your How-To book includes the same helpers or different ones?"

Highlight one feature a partnership noticed—I highlighted the observation that the steps were numbered—and add this to the chart of How-To helpers.

"Cameron and Domini found something really interesting." I picked up their text and showed it to the class. "Their author used numbers for each step. Do you see how she writes 1, 2, 3, and so on? Let's include that in our list of How-To helpers!" This became the fourth item on the list.

HOW-TO HELPERS
....

1. A title that says this will be a How-To book
2. A list of the things we'll need
3. Pictures that teach us what to do
4. *Numbers for each step*

"You found so many ways authors help us read these How-To books!" I referred to each item on the chart in turn and asked children to put their thumbs up if they had found that feature.

To keep the lesson short, I often pre-make charts such as this one, which aren't elicited from children. Then I simply uncover the chart at this point. Once you introduce a chart, return to it often, adding to it and showing children how you follow the chart's guidance. You may want to give the children personal copies of these charts or turn them into personal checklists so they can (in this instance) tick off which of these features they've included in their books.

This is a challenging, open-ended activity, but your children should be able to launch into it immediately. They could easily work for fifteen minutes rather than the usual three, and you may decide it's important and enthralling enough to give them extra time. If so, be sure to tell them beforehand that this isn't a normal minilesson, that just this once they'll have more time for their investigation.

Keep in mind, however, that your kids will also benefit from spending just a few minutes gleaning an impression of the conventions used in How-To writing.

In this teaching sequence, we've made a list and then used that list as a rubric to guide our reflections on our work. This shows children the ways in which a criterion can play a role in guiding work.

Link

Send the children off to revise How-To books they've already written so that they include these features.

"Today, I know some of you are revising your How-To books and others are starting on new ones. Remember that when you write a How-To book, it's smart to check it by trying it out on a reader. For example, when I tried to follow Sam's somersault book and Troyquon tried out his pizza book, they both realized they had confusing parts, and they went back and fixed these parts. Be sure you find the confusing parts in your first drafts. Meanwhile, use our list of helpers and make sure you give your readers helpers like those on our list."

It is very important that the teaching you do in minilessons and conferences needs to make a lasting impact on children. In today's link you not only remind children that the content applies to any time they ever write How-To books . . . you also remind them of lessons they have learned on previous days.

TIME TO CONFER

For children who've aspired to write beautiful literary stories, the effort to write straight, clear, how-to texts may seem less demanding. You could convene these youngsters into a small-group strategy lesson and raise the level of challenge by pointing out that, so far, they've *recorded* steps in procedures that are already well known. They might instead *invent* steps in areas of personal expertise. That is, its one thing to record the steps in making an omelet, it's another thing to invent a way to welcome new children into one's classroom. If you want to raise the challenge level for your writers, you could suggest topics like these:

- How to turn your sofa into a spaceship
- How to help the class have a great book talk
- How to find a book you LOVE
- How to make a magnificent castle out of blocks
- How to make your mother (or your teacher) more apt to say yes when you ask for a favor
- How to keep yourself from laughing when you're supposed to be serious
- How to help your Dad have the best birthday ever

These conferences in *The Conferring Handbook* may be especially helpful today:

- "Make a Mental Movie of Yourself Following Your Directions to Test Them for Clarity"
- "What Will You Write in Your Table of Contents?"
- "If There's No Punctuation, When I Read Your Report It Sounds Like Gobbledygook"

Also, if you have *Conferring with Primary Writers*, you may want to refer to the conferences in part six.

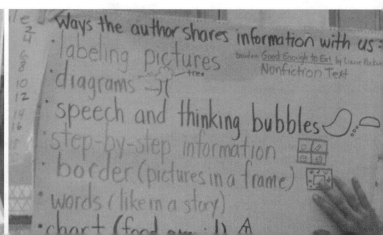

Celebrate writers who've used the class How-To helpers in their writing. Reread the chart, item by item, while children check to see if they followed each suggestion.

"Writers many of you used the How-To helpers that we listed earlier today. And I saw some of you checking that list as you wrote, using the list as a writing helper! That's really smart. Let's all do that.

"Right now, put the book you worked on today on the carpet in front of you. Let's read our chart, item by item, and check to see whether our writing contains that item."

With my pointer, I indicated the title of the chart, and the class read it in unison. Then I pointed to the first item, and the class again read in unison. "So check your book. Did you do this—thumbs up—or not—thumbs down." We read the other items on the chart together, with children giving a thumbs up or thumbs down to signify whether they'd included this helper in their book.

> ### HOW-TO HELPERS
> ....
> 1.   A title that says this will be a How-To book
> 2.   A list of the things we'll need
> 3.   Pictures that teach us what to do
> 4.   Numbers for each step

Once you've reread the chart and children have noticed which items on it they do and do not incorporate into their drafts, suggest that children make plans to revise.

"I'm wondering, did any of you get ideas for what you might want to revise or add? If so, write yourself a sticky note."

"Writers, I'm hoping you learned that lists like these can remind you of ways to improve writing. I use shopping lists to remind me of what to buy at the grocery store—and lists that we make during the writing workshop to remind me of how to write well."

As children convene, make sure they each have a few sticky notes and a pen.

There is a saying, "Give someone a fish, they eat for a day. Teach someone how to fish, they eat for a lifetime." I'm not just reminding children to incorporate the features of non-narrative texts that we have studied, I'm teaching them to use the charts we make as guides to help them remember all we've studied together.

I've given the children a lot of scaffolding—they have all used the list we made as a class to guide them to reflect on what they have and haven't done and to aspire to do more. Now I name the lesson I hope they've learned about classroom lists. In a minute, I'll set them up to do similar work involving a second classroom list, only this time they'll work more independently.

If children have used features of How-To writing that weren't in the unit, add one or two to the list.

"Did any of you use helpers that weren't on the list?"

Nicole held her writing up and pointed at her picture.

"That's right. I promised Nicole that I'd tell the rest of you about something really smart she did. Nicole got the idea to write some words under each of her pictures." See the caption in the lower left-hand drawing in Figure IV-1. "She wrote what people call *captions*. Here, for example, under her picture she wrote 'These are the flowers that I love.' Let's add Nicole's idea to our chart."

HOW-TO HELPERS

....

1. A title that says this will be a How-To book
2. A list of the things we'll need
3. Pictures that teach us what to do
4. Numbers for each step
5. *Captions under the pictures*

"And Napoleon helped us in another way. He wrote labels for some of the important parts of his picture so we will know what they are." Napoleon held up his page. "You see on this page, he wrote labels so that we would know more. He wrote *lyts*, and over here he wrote *lader*." I pointed to the labels. "So writers, as you continue to work on your writing, keep thinking about places where you can help your readers. I'll add 'labels' to the chart while you get started writing."

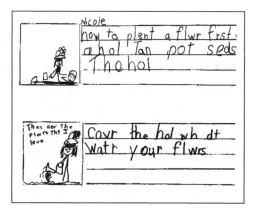

Fig. IV-1 Nicole

How to plant a flower
First dig a hole and put seeds in the hole.
Cover the hole with dirt.
Water your flowers.

Caption: These are the flowers
that I love.

IF CHILDREN NEED MORE TIME

When you point out text features that occur in How-To texts, some children will immediately begin incorporating these into their own writing and others will need more explicit instructions. In later minilessons or small group strategy lessons, you might:

▶ Listen for children's observations when they study published How-To books from your basket of example texts, and turn their observations into minilessons or future "mid-workshop teaching points." Children will probably notice the playfulness in these books such as times when a How-To book about mixing colors displays each numbered step in a different color. Show a variety of ways authors are playful and invite children to be similarly inventive.

▶ Highlight the importance of conventions by copying a page from *The Pumpkin Book* without the pictures, numbered steps, and so on, and letting children experience the resulting confusion.

▶ Show children ways they might make their pictures more instructive. This might include teaching them about captions, labels, exact observations, use of arrows and numbers, zoomed-in diagrams, and so on.

▶ Study ways authors anticipate difficulties readers will encounter, adding warnings (such as "Be careful not to spill this"). Sometimes writers add these cautionary comments in little boxes.

▶ Talk about the endings of these books. Often they end with a twist. A book on making soup ends with, "Then eat it!" A book on making a flower arrangement ends with the flowers being delivered to someone.

▶ Explicitly teach children how writers use charts and rubrics to guide our writing. For example, teach children that if they are unsure what to do to improve their draft and there is no teacher on hand, a chart such as "How-To Helpers" can be a source of reminders. Demonstrate how a writer might go about using the chart. As you do this, keep in mind that your classroom charts and rubrics are all forms of How-To writing!

My first book, *Lessons from a Child,* was the story of the education I received from a young girl named Susie Sable. Every day for two years, I observed Susie as she wrote, and from this close study of one child I learned most of what I know about teaching writing. There will be times when you want to assess the patterns and issues you see across your class as a whole, but there will be other days when you decide to focus your assessment on a child or two. It's interesting, for example, to look closely at Zachary's and Ari's books.

Zachary spells well for a kindergarten English-language learner, but his concern for spelling may explain why, in both of the versions he's written of how to play tennis, he uses a constrained form.

In one version, he lists what a person needs to play tennis. [*Fig. IV-2*]

Then Zachary was taught to stretch his How-To book across a sequence of pages. In his new draft, every page still follows a strict pattern. "First you need a racket, second you need two people to tennis."

Zachary has trouble with verbs and pronouns, both predictable problem areas for English-language learners. [*Fig. IV-3*]

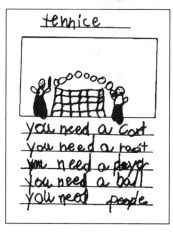

You need a court
You need a racket
You need a player
You need a ball
You need people

Fig. IV-2 Zachary

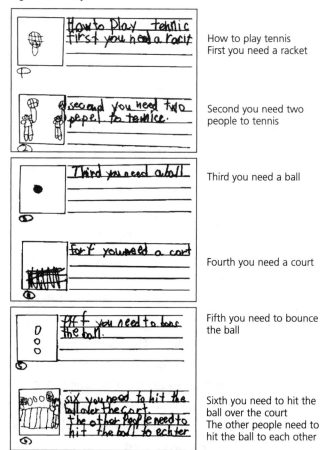

How to play tennis
First you need a racket

Second you need two
people to tennis

Third you need a ball

Fourth you need a court

Fifth you need to bounce
the ball

Sixth you need to hit the
ball over the court
The other people need to
hit the ball to each other

Fig. IV-3 Zachary

Ari has a lot of control over English syntax. It's unusual that a child who is this new to writing writes sentences that span four pages and contains many subordinate clauses. [*Fig. IV-4*]

At this juncture, take your children's work home. Reflect on their progress with this rubric in mind:

Assessment Rubric for Nonfiction How-To Writing	Has achieved this	Shows progress towards this	Needs help to get started
The writing gives instructions or directions on how to do something.			
The picture illustrates the steps in the directions.			
The writing follows an appropriate sequence.			
The writing demonstrates efforts to make the text coherent, either with numbers or transitional words.			
The writing and/or pictures include text features associated with this genre.			

Before long, you need to either end the How-To portion of this unit or send children back to write more of these texts. Decide which path you'll follow today. You may decide that writing How-To books is challenging for your children that you'd rather the cycle through this genre several times instead of moving on to other forms of nonfiction writing. Your kids could write a slew of How-To books while you teach lessons described under "If Children Need More Time."

Alternatively, you may decide your children will soon be ready for the challenge of writing "All-About" information books. Because How-To texts follow the chronological sequence of an activity, they don't put as many organizational demands on writers as do All-About texts. In this book, we soon move children on to write All-About books.

To make orange juice, you
squeeze the orange
and you put it in a jar
and when you want a drink, you
put it in a glass
mmm! This is good

Fig. IV-4 Ari

REVISING: LEARNING FROM A VARIETY OF HOW-TO WRITING

GETTING READY

▶ Gail Gibbons' *The Pumpkin Book*
▶ Many examples of How-To texts (memos, game instructions, etc.
⊚ See CD-ROM for resources

I'VE SOMETIMES COMPARED *a teacher of writing to a circus performer who gets plates spinning on sticks. She gets one plate spinning, then another, then another, and runs between the poles, each holding a spinning plate, giving just a touch here and a touch there, enough to keep everything in motion.*

Your plates are all spinning now. One child is rereading her draft to visualize herself following each step she's laid out. Another is adding captions under his pictures. A few children are using checklists as guides for revision.

Your first goal is to encourage children to use all they know to plan, draft, and revise their How-To writing. But you also want to raise the level of your children's learning to broaden their sense of How-To writing so that they realize that, although How-To texts often come in the specific format they've studied, this isn't always the case. You want your children to begin seeing How-To texts everywhere: in the directions a pharmacist writes on a medicine bottle, in the sign on an elevator informing passengers of what to do in case of an emergency, on the inside cover of a Monopoly game. You want children to understand that one genre of writing blends with others. Some poems are variations on How-To writing, and some picture book pages read rather like How-To texts.

Once children begin seeing How-To texts everywhere, they will develop a wider sense of the options that are (and are not) available to them as authors of this genre. Remind children that the world is full of a huge variety of How-To texts and that they can learn by studying them.

THE MINILESSON

Connection

Remind the children that they've used charts to guide revisions. Suggest they can also use How-To texts they find in the world to remind them of what writers do.

"I know you guys used charts yesterday to remember things we've noticed about How-To writing and that some of you have used the charts to plan your revisions." I show a sticky note holding one child's revision plans. "You're smart to revise your writing because we'll publish soon. Just as charts remind us of our goals, examples of what other authors have written also remind us of our goals."

Tell children about a memo from the front office that qualifies as How-To text and share your realization that the world is full of many kinds of How-To texts, all of which deserve to be studied.

"The front office sent us a memo this morning reminding us of the procedures to follow if we're at gym or lunch when there's a fire drill."

"And reading this over, I realized that even though it doesn't *look* like the How-To writing we've been studying or writing, it's still a How-To (some people call it a procedural) text, and we could be learning from it as writers. Let's read it and see if it can teach us some pointers. And then let's remember that How-To writing comes in many different shapes, sizes, and formats, and we need to see this kind of writing everywhere and be ready to learn from it."

My wording reflects that I've decided to move this class on soon to write All-About texts, and I'm heading towards an end of this How-To portion of the unit. If you decide to lengthen the How-To component of this unit, postpone this minilesson until you are close to the end.

I tell children that the world is full of How-To texts and they come in all shapes and sizes. Mostly, I make the big point—the one point that will pull the minilesson together—that just as we use charts as reminders of goals for our writing, we can also use exemplars.

Teach

Read the memo aloud as an example of procedural text.

"So listen to the memo, look at it (I'll show it on the overhead projector), and see if you can learn from it. The memo is headed 'Fire Drill Instructions,' and it starts:"

> I want to remind you that if there is a fire drill when you are at gym or lunch, you are to go immediately down the East staircase. You'll walk behind the third-grade classes along Barkers Street. . . .

Tell children two lessons you learned from this text. One concerns the variety of How-To texts in the world, the other is that many texts include cautionary notes.

"I started to read this. Then I stopped. I realized that How-To writing doesn't always come written in steps with numbers and a picture next to it. It can be written that way, but it doesn't need to be. I also noticed that at the end of these directions there was a warning set out in a special box on the side: 'Remember, even if you don't have coats, you cannot go back to your classroom!'"

"I realized that a lot of procedural writing, a lot of How-To writing, includes cautionary notes (or warnings). Sometimes the warning is set apart with a special font, special letters, and sometimes it's merged into the rest of the text, but there is often this important advice or warning."

Show other How-To texts that include cautionary notes.

"In this How-To book the author includes a little warning box and it says, 'Have an adult help you!'"

"And listen again to Gail Gibbons' *The Pumpkin Book*. Number 5 says, 'Be careful and ALWAYS carve away from yourself.' I guess she worried that if she just said, 'Cut along the lines,' someone could hold the knife wrong and cut a finger."

"So today, some of you may want to add a warning to one of your How-To books, and you may want to think about doing some procedural writing that isn't in the How-To format we've studied."

If you can keep an overhead projector set up at the front of your meeting area, you'll find it invaluable. But if using an overhead requires wheeling an ungainly machine into place, find other ways to enlarge texts.

There may not be a lot of new things to learn from studying most of these texts, but one will be the cautionary notes they often include.

Notice that I don't hesitate to use vocabulary that is probably new for this group of K–1 children, but that I tuck synonyms for the new words alongside them when I do.

I could have passed out How-To books and had the children search through them to find other instances in which there were cautionary notes, but I decided active engagement wouldn't take the children very far intellectually. Writers of this genre don't need to get good at searching through books for evidence of cautionary notes! Therefore, I did the searching myself (I could have had a small group do it the day before and tell me what they found) and saved the active engagement for more ambitious and rewarding work.

Remind the children of the larger point. Just as charts can guide them, so too can example texts.

"But most of all, always remember that we can make our writing better by using charts to guide us and by noticing that the world is full of the kind of writing we want to do. We need to live like magnets, pulling in things about whatever genre—whatever kind of writing—we're trying to do."

Active Engagement

Pass out an array of How-To (procedural) texts and ask the children to study these with a partner or small group and learn from what they see.

"Now I'm going to pass out some How-To texts that don't look like the How-To books we've been studying. You'll see these are all directions—instructions—procedures—of one kind or another. Some of what I'm passing out is only partly How-To writing and partly something else. Will you and the people near you study the text I give you and notice what the author has done? Perhaps the author will surprise you and give you ideas for what you could do as you begin to prepare your writing for publication." I handed out an array of How-To texts. (See CD-ROM for suggestions.)

Children read and talked for a few minutes.

Link

Tell writers that the expanded collection of How-To writing will be available to them anytime. Ask them to think, in their mind, of what they'll do today and to signal when they're ready.

"Writers, I'm going to put all our How-To texts together in this basket. If you want to continue studying them, they'll be here. When you leave today, pay very close attention to everything around you and see if you find any more How-To texts. If you go shopping, see if you can find any at the store. If you go to a restaurant, see what's there, and then do the same at home. See what you can learn from those authors, and if you want to bring something in to add to our collection, that'd be great."

"For now, it's time to get started. Think in your mind of exactly what you'll do first today. Thumbs up when you are ready to start."

I'm summarizing today's teaching point and yesterday's in a way which is cumulative. I believe it will be easier for children to remember and use these pointers because I've shown how they go together. We can make our writing better by using charts to guide us and by learning from exemplar texts.

Try to dole these out with an eye toward kids' ability to read. If your kindergartners or first graders are still emerging readers, instead of passing them out, you may decide to show some of particular texts to the class, reading a tiny bit aloud, and have children tell their partner what they notice.

You needn't solicit their observations. It's time to write.

TIME TO CONFER

Today you may want to carry a few texts with you when you confer and to refer to those texts often. Earlier, you carried literature with you because you were teaching children to learn from mentor authors. See "Can We Study What This Author Did and Let Her Teach Us Some Lessons?" from the *Conferring with Primary Writers* book. Today, if you carry two Gail Gibbons books, The Pumpkin Book and Apples, and if you bookmark the How-To sections of each, you'll find them very helpful.

- If a few children seem ready, suggest they join you in studying Gibbons' writing. Children can easily notice and emulate the structure "lists with a twist." The endings are often a little special.
- Don't explain parts of speech to five-year-olds, but children can learn that lists are characterized by parallel structure. Each item in these lists "sounds the same"; the instructions all "match." For example, "First you need to get . . . "; "Second you need to buy . . ."; "Third you need to mix . . ." In Gibbons' writing, each new step begins with an imperative (don't tell this to kids, let them discover it) such as "take a knife," "draw the design," "pack down the soil."
- Point out that writers sometimes cross out words they don't need. The same text could be written "Get . . .", "Buy . . .", "Mix. . . ."

These conferences in *The Conferring Handbook* may be especially helpful today:

- *"Make a Mental Movie of Yourself Following Your Directions to Test Them for Clarity"*
- *"What Will You Write in Your Table of Contents?"*
- *"If There's No Punctuation, When I Read Your Report It Sounds Like Gobbledygook"*

Also, if you have *Conferring with Primary Writers*, you may want to refer to the conferences in part six.

AFTER-THE WORKSHOP SHARE

Tell the children the story of a classmate who noticed something in a How-To book and tried to do it in his or her own writing.

"Today, writers, I want you to hear about writers in this room who noticed something an author did and tried the same technique."

"I've asked three writers to share. Each will first read and talk about something he or she found in the work of another author, then the writer will read what he or she did as a result."

Danya, a kindergartener, began. She said, "I saw the warning in *The Pumpkin Book* ["Always carve away from yourself"], and I read my library card book and put a warning at the end." Then she read the last two pages aloud. [*Fig. V-1*]

Michael, the class gardener, wrote about how to grow tomatoes. "I put arrows in different directions, just like they did on the airplane card. These are arrows that go in different directions, so I wanted to try that also." He pointed to his page. "I made a down arrow over here because you need to place the stick down into the ground, and I made a sideways arrow here because you need to tie the tomato plant to the stick."

Carolina was the last to share. "I like the end of this book." She read from *How to Make Salsa*, by Jamie Lucero. "I like the last page. 'It's salsa party time.' It reminds me of writing stories. So I can write a How-To book and story all together." Carolina then read the last page of her *How to Make Play Dough*: "Have fun, and don't worry if you lose some. You can always make more."

---

oftr you eit your
LiBUrycrD you CAN
tAKeowt AS mANY
BooKs AS you Want
AND you CAN tAke
LoTs AND LoTs OF Books
oWt FOR Feu
WiTh that LiBUrRcrD
AND IF You
LoS your LiBUryoo
you Just ta
them AND they
WiLU gIV you a NuDr
oNé

After you get your library card you can take out as many books as you want and you can take lots and lot of books out for free with that libra card. And if you lose your library ca you just tell them and they will giv you another one.

But you HAV too
Look iN the
BACK too See WiNU too
retrN it
AND IF You
retrN
the BooK Lat
you NYt too PAY
10 sisu

But you have to look in the back to see when to return it and if you return the book late you need to p ten cents.

Fig. V-1 Danya

EDITING: USING PERIODS, PARENTHESES, AND COLONS

GETTING READY

- How-To Helpers checklists
- Overhead projector
- Overhead transparency of How-To page from *Apples* by Gail Gibbons
- Multiple copies of a pre-selected student book
- See CD-ROM for resources

MANY OF YOU WILL HAVE DECIDED, *as we did, to divide this unit in half and to devote the first two weeks to How-To writing and the next two weeks to informational texts. If your timetable is the same as ours, you now need to encourage your writers to fix up their work for publication. They will have been revising their How-To books all along. In this session you'll want to ask your children to select one text to send to the publishing center. Once they've selected a book to publish, they'll need to double-check their revisions of that book and then turn their attention to editing. Remind them to use the strategies they've discovered to improve their spelling, and spotlight some of the punctuation they're apt to use in How-To books.*

Connection

Tell your children that a celebration will be held on a later day. They need to select a text to publish and use class charts to guide them in improving it.

"Writers," Laurie said, waiting for the children's eyes to rest on her, "I know you've been revising all your How-To texts. That's good because we'll each publish one on Friday. This means that, as always, you'll need to select one of your texts to send to the publishing center, where it'll get typed up so it can become part of our library. Before you send it to be published, make sure you've done everything you can to make it a great book."

"I've turned our charts into check-off sheets, and you can use them as guides for revision."

You'll want to decide whether you can recruit enough help to have your children's published work typed. If you can do this, you'll find these texts become very popular reading material for the class.

REVISION CHECKLIST FOR HOW-TO BOOKS

	Yes	Not yet
A title that says this will be a How-To book		
A list of things we'll need.		
Pictures that teach us what to do.		
Numbers for each step.		
Captions under the pictures.		

You taught them how to do these things in earlier minilessons. Keep in mind that almost every chart you and the class make could be turned into a checklist, with each child having a copy in his or her writing folder. This is a concrete way to bring home the message that charts exist for a purpose. They are not intended as merely wallpaper for your classroom!

Tell the children you want to teach one new thing that How-To writers use: punctuation.

"But I want to teach one new thing that How-To writers think about, and that's punctuation."

Teach

Remind your children that earlier they learned about ellipses from Angela Johnson. Tell them that today they'll study the punctuation How-To authors often use.

"Remember that we noticed Angela Johnson used dot, dot, dot a lot in her books, and many of you decided to include dot, dot, dot—ellipses—in your writing?"

"Writers, authors of How-To books have a few kinds of punctuation they often use."

Use the overhead projector to enlarge one page that uses the punctuation you decide to highlight. Ask children to name the punctuation they notice to their partner.

"Let's study what these are and why an author uses them because you may want to use the same punctuation in *your* How-To books (as well as in other writing you do from now on)." Laurie put a transparency on the overhead projector. "Look at this page about making an apple pie from the book *Apples*. I'm going to read this page to you, and I want you and your partner to notice the punctuation Gail Gibbons uses and see if you can figure out the job this punctuation is doing."

Laurie read:

Mix 1/2 cup (118 ml) brown sugar and
1/4 teaspoon (1.23 ml) salt.

"Let me stop there. Tell your partner what punctuation you notice and what job it does." Everyone broke into conversation.

Your children had great success learning ellipses. By recalling this, you suggest today's lesson will have equal payoffs for them.

In How-To texts, one often sees parentheses, the colon, and dashes. Of course, there aren't kinds of punctuation that occur only and uniquely in one genre.

You aren't expecting mastery. You are raising your students' consciousness and luring them to think about punctuation—which will have many payoffs.

You may question whether children who can't figure out periods should be thinking about parentheses. The truth is, parentheses are easier and more thrilling for children. Learning parentheses can fire up children to care about punctuation, which can, in turn, help with more basic punctuation.

Reconvene the class. Say what you heard them say (or hope you heard them say) about periods and, in this instance, parentheses.

"I heard you saying smart things. All of you noticed that Gail Gibbons used periods at the end of one idea. Periods say, 'Take a little breath when you read this.' If she didn't have a period, everything in her sentence could get mixed up. Each writer here should have periods in his or her writing. You need to read your writing aloud, and when you get to the end of an idea, when it's time to breathe, put in a period."

"Many of you also noticed that Gibbons uses these marks [( )]. Some of you called them big curls, and they do look like that! They're actually called *parentheses*. Can you say that?"

The class chimed in: "Parentheses. Parentheses."

Laurie continued, "Writers use parentheses when they want to pause for one second and add one little point, or to say one more thing."

Give children more examples of How-To texts that use parentheses.

"So I could write these instructions on cleaning out the fish tank:
- Empty out the dirty water (first put the fish in a safe place).
- Rinse off the gravel."

"Or I could write these directions for making chocolate cookies:
- Preheat the oven (350 degrees).
- Put the pan of cookies into the oven (don't burn yourself)."

Active Engagement

Recruit the class to help one child add periods into her How-To writing. Give each partnership a copy of a child's text and read the text aloud. Ask children to work with their partners to add periods.

"I'm wondering if you can help Jacqueline reread her writing and add periods to it."

"I'm going to read it aloud. Will you follow along on a copy of her text, making a period where you think she needs to add one?" [*Fig. VI-1*]

Obviously you won't highlight periods if you teach second graders who no longer need to notice them. On the other hand, if your children do need to be reminded of the importance of periods, you can pretend you overheard children noticing periods whether or not you actually did.

Use your hands as parentheses, curling around your voice when you read these directions.

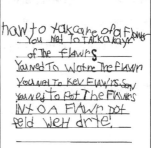

How to Take Care of a Flower
(That's a title, the name of the book, and you underline that.)
You need to take care of the flowers (.)
You need to water the flowers (.)
You need to give flowers sun (.)
You need to put the flowers into a flower pot filled with dirt.

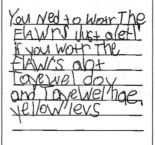

You need to water the Flowers just a little (.)
If you water the flowers a lot they will die and they will have yellow leaves (.)

Fig. VI-1   Jacqueline

If it's an inconvenience to make copies for the children, they can pretend to have a copy in front of them and pretend to add dots in the necessary places.

Reread it, doing this yourself, so they can check their efforts.

"I'll do it again. This time, I'll add periods into my copy." Laurie stood before the overhead projector, dry-erase pen in hand. "See if you agree with me about where the periods go." This time Laurie read the text, pausing long enough for the kids to be the first to say, "Period." Then she added the end punctuation before proceeding.

Now recruit the children to add parentheses. Again, read the text aloud, this time asking them to find instances where parentheses will help.

"Jacqueline also decided she had better add in exactly how much water she means when she says that they just need a little water. She wants to add that half a cup is a good amount. I'll reread her direction, and will you and your partner decide where she could add that little more information, and whether there's some punctuation she could use?" Laurie again read the text aloud, this time adding the parenthetical comment orally and then into the written text.

Link

Send children off to publish their writing. Remind them of the steps they will need to follow.

"So writers, you have a lot to do today: 1. Pick the piece that you'll publish. Some of you have done that already. 2. Reread it, checking off which items from our charts you've done. If you get ideas for more you can do to make it your very best, do it. 3. Check your spellings. Make sure you've spelled words on our word wall correctly. 4. Check your punctuation. Remember to see if you need to use parentheses. Off you go!"

You'll be reading this aloud so your voice is making the job a lot easier for your children. If you are teaching second graders and want to increase the challenge, ask each child to reread the text on his or her own, adding punctuation.

TIME TO CONFER

If you find yourself saying the same thing from child to child, ask for the class's attention and offer mid-workshop advice. As you move among individuals, you'll probably find many children have not used the minilesson on periods (let alone parentheses). Perhaps you'll nudge the children to reread, checking for periods in the directions, or to use the word wall to check spellings, or blends. See conference cited at right. When you confer with children about conventions, remember that if you intervene in a way that improves the writing but doesn't help the writer do better work another time with another piece, you've accomplished nothing. Don't aim for the piece to be perfect if the cost of a child becoming utterly dependent on you to microcheck his every move. Aim for the writer to learn a few new things with each text he writes.

These conferences in *The Conferring Handbook* may be especially helpful today:

- ▶ *"If There's No Punctuation, When I Read Your Report It Sounds Like Gobbledygook"*
- ▶ *"Famous Writers Use Periods to Tell Readers When to Stop"*

Also, if you have *Conferring with Primary Writers*, you may want to refer to the conferences in part six.

Remind the class of the things they need to do to prepare for publication.

"I've loved watching the hard work you are doing as you get ready to publish. You are looking to see if your writing makes sense, giving readers helpers, and you are checking to be sure you have spelled as many words as you can correctly."

Choose a child to read his or her piece and invite the entire class to help him or her check that it is clear and includes How-To helpers.

"Let's join Bryant in making sure that he is ready to publish his writing. We'll check this in two ways. First we'll see if we can follow his directions and do what he wants us to do. Let's listen carefully to Bryant as he reads." Laurie turned to Bryant. "After you read each page, we're going to imagine doing what you describe. While we imagine doing that step, show us your picture."

Bryant read aloud, *How to Play the Piano.* [*Fig. VI-2*]

Stop and ask the children to talk quickly to their partners about the helpers that Bryant has used so far.

Most of the "helpers" in a How-To book are evident within the first two pages. Therefore, after reading just a snippet of the text, Laurie said, "Would you turn and tell your partner the helpers Bryant has used so far?" The room erupted with conversation, and Laurie moved among the youngsters, listening in.

Remind children that they can all try what Bryant has tried with their own writing.

"Remember, you can all use the same helpers Bryant has used in your own writing!"

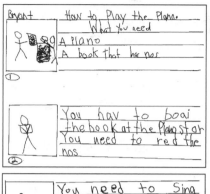
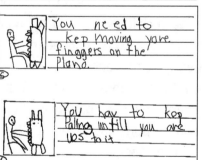

How to Play the Piano
What You Need.
A piano.
A book that has notes.

You have to buy the book at the piano store. You need to read the notes.

You need to sing the song.

You need to put your hands on the piano. Make sure that your hands stay there.

You need to keep moving your fingers on the piano.

You have to keep playing until you are used to it.

Fig. VI-2 Bryant

It makes sense that children listen to see if they can follow the directions and then step back and ask, "Were there features that helped me understand?"

Laurie emphasizes revision by saying that writers continually try their directions to see if people can follow them.

If your children haven't fully assimilated these concepts, don't despair. This is really a double-decker minilesson.

▶ You could teach children to reread slowly when checking for spelling errors and to point under each word, asking, "Is this right?" You could show children that if a word seems wrong, it helps to ask, "Is any part of it right?" and in this way hone in on the troublesome section, rewriting that portion of the word differently.

▶ You could devote several minilessons to the importance of end punctuation. Don't expect that you'll ever be able to fully explain the rules for differentiating fragments from sentences to five- and six-year-olds, but as children's texts begin to involve more sentences on a single page, it will be increasingly important for them to use punctuation as best they can.

▶ You could teach children to use a colon before a list. Many directions have a colon just prior to a list of ingredients. Granted, most of us adults don't use colons when we write, and this is certainly not crucial information for children who can't yet use periods correctly, but in fact it's far easier to use the colon than to discern sentence boundaries! When children use the colon well, they get a kick out of punctuation, and both their self-concept and their concept of punctuation can soar.

▶ You will want to hold a small-scale author's celebration to reinforce the information of the unit, to signal the start of new work, and to cheer the children on. You may want to invite your children's upper-grade reading buddies, parents, and caregivers to class. The children could hold teaching "workshops" in different corners of the room. In each workshop, a few children could take turns reading their text aloud. If there is time enough, the learners could ask the writers more questions about their topics. (For more details about how this celebration might go, turn to the CD-ROM.)

ASSESSMENT

At the end of the first part of this unit, you will want to take your children's writing home and assess what your children have done. You will want to use the rubric that was developed in Session IV, but you will have some additional criteria in mind.

Assessment Rubric for How-To Writing	Has achieved this	Shows progress toward this	Needs help to get started in this
The writing gives instructions or directions on how to do something.			
The picture illustrates the steps in the directions.			
The writing follows an appropriate sequence.			
The writing demonstrates some way of making the text coherent, by either numbers or transitional words.			
The writing and/or pictures include text features associated with this genre.			
The writing includes punctuation—periods, parentheses, and colons			

INTRODUCING ALL-ABOUT BOOKS

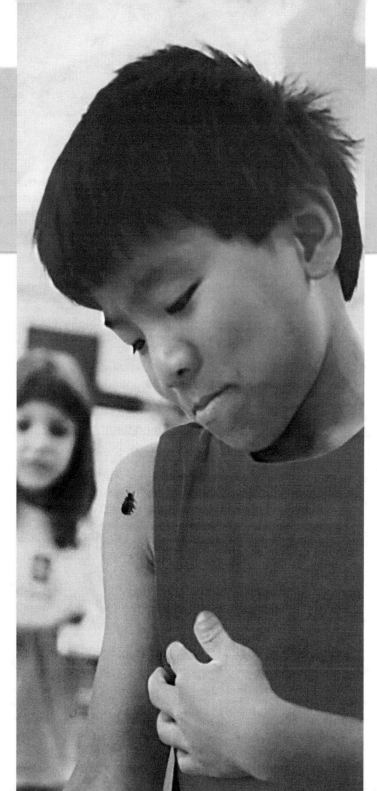

GETTING READY

- Before this session, you may want to have a small celebration (see the CD-ROM)
- *The Pumpkin Book*, by Gail Gibbons. Ideally, make transparencies of selected pages, each page addressing a different subtopic.
- Overhead projector
- A collection of published All-About books that you can distribute, one for every partnership. Ideally, select books that have an All-About title, a table of contents, and chapters. It isn't crucial that your children be able to read these books.
- Chart paper and marker
- A book your children know well that has chapters (perhaps *Poppleton* or *My Father's Dragon*)
- All-About topic paper
- See CD-ROM for resources

THIS MINILESSON MARKS THE *beginning of Part 2 of this unit and will launch your children on a study of informational (or "All-About," or "teaching") writing. This minilesson, then, functions rather like the first minilesson in a new unit. Your goal is to give children an overall impression of what they'll write, kindle their enthusiasm for the work they'll undertake, and help them choose a topic that they'll write about for the next few weeks. You don't want them to begin writing their own All-About books today. Instead, today's writing workshop gives the children time to study published All-About books. You'll remind them that it's always wise to learn from the pros. When my son wants to learn a skateboarding trick, he goes to the local skate park and watches kids who "are almost professional." Then he tries to do what they do. Similarly, we tell young writers, "We need to study how the pros write teaching books."*

Your children will have already studied one page of The Pumpkin Book, *the page that gives directions for carving a pumpkin. In this minilesson, your children will study the whole text of* The Pumpkin Book *to glimpse the overall structure of informational writing.*

THE MINILESSON

Connection

Remind children that they've learned to write texts that teach readers how to do something. Now they'll learn to write books that teach readers all about a subject.

"Writers, we have all written books that teach readers how to do something. We learned from Gail Gibbons, who, you remember, wrote a page about how to carve a pumpkin."

"Today I want to tell you that writers can also teach readers 'all about' a subject. For the next few weeks, we'll learn how to write All-About books."

Ideally, our teaching scaffolds children so they are carried from easier to more complex work, as in this instance.

Teach

Remind the children that when they want to do a new kind of writing, it helps to study texts similar to those they want to write.

"My son, Evan, wants to learn skateboarding tricks, so yesterday he went to the skate park and studied what the older kids do. Then he came home and tried to do the tricks he'd seen the pros doing. Writers, like skateboarders, often learn by seeing what the pros do. And so if you and I want to write All-About books, one of the first things we need to do is to study All-About books written by the pros. We'll do that today."

"Let's start by studying *The Pumpkin Book*. One page is a How-To page, but the *whole book* could be called *All About Pumpkins*. Let's notice how this kind of book goes and list what we notice across our fingers."

Let children hear your thinking as you begin.

"Okay. First, the title, *The Pumpkin Book*. I'm noticing that the title of the book gives the reader a clue that this will be an All-About book. It doesn't say, *The Story of a Boy and His Pumpkin*, or *How to Pick a Pumpkin*, or *Kinds of Pumpkins*. Instead it says, *The Pumpkin Book*, which gives me the idea this book is on the big topic of pumpkins."

The injunction to collect parallel entities (in this case, observations about All-About books) and to list them across one's fingers sets children up for some of the mental work—identifying parallel points and elaborating on each—that is fundamental to most non-narrative writing.

I could have asked, "What do you notice?", but I have a few features in mind to spotlight. I try not to ask questions if I already know the answer I want. By showing what the title doesn't say, I help highlight what I notice about the title.

Holding one finger, I reiterated, "So the first thing I notice in All-About writing is that the title gives readers a clue that this will be an All-About book and, at least in this instance, that it will be all about a big topic." With my hands I showed that this is what in an earlier unit we referred to as a "watermelon topic," but I don't use the words lest some of the children get confused about pumpkins turning into watermelons!

Notice aloud that All-About books are divided into parts.

I turned the page. "Now I notice the book has different sections. Look at this! This section is about the different kinds of pumpkins." I flipped past that page, surveying the next page I flipped to. "This section is about the plants on which pumpkins grow. And here is a section on the history of the pumpkin. And this section of the book is about pumpkins and Halloween. We already know that there is the 'How to Carve a Pumpkin' page in this book, but here is another How-To page, 'How to Dry Your Pumpkin Seeds.'"

"So I notice that this book has different sections, like different chapters. All the sections, or chapters, fit under the big topic of pumpkins, but each section is about something different."

List the features you've noticed in an All-About book.

I flipped up the page on my pad of chart paper to reveal a clean page and began to list the features we'd mentioned that occur in All-About books.

We want children to realize that our teaching on any one day is always meant to influence tomorrow and next month. So it is important that our teaching be cumulative. That is, in March, we'll refer back to phrases ("watermelon topic") that were key in September, October, and November. In this instance, I use a gesture rather than a term to recall an earlier lesson.

This observation is an absolutely crucial one. One of the biggest challenges children will encounter when writing in this genre is that they need to categorize their information. Here, I suggest they sort information into pages which are ear-marked for different sub-topics.

I wish Gibbons' books had chapters and a table of contents, but they don't. But since they are perfect examples in every way but this, I stretch things a bit and describe her books as having "sections" (which I am sort of equating with chapters).

Don't notice and list too many features. Lists are more helpful when they aren't overly long.

ALL-ABOUT BOOKS OFTEN HAVE

. . . .

▸ A big All-About title

▸ A How-To page

▸ Chapters or sections

Active Engagement

Give each partnership an All-About book and ask them to check if their book has these features. What other features do they notice?

"I'm going to give you and your partner another All-About book; will you investigate and see if *your* All-About book has these same features? Check whether," I referred to the list, "your book has a big All-About title that signals to readers that this book will teach them all about a big topic."

"An All-About book is more like a whole hand than a single finger. It's big, and it has parts that go into it. See if you can see the big title," I touched the palm of my hand, "and see if you can see smaller sections or chapters," I touched my fingers. "How are the sections divided up," I spread my fingers apart, "so they don't all glob together? Turn and talk with your partner."

Convene your children and gather their observations about All-About books.

I pointed to the chart. "Thumbs up if your book had a big All-About title?" Most thumbs went up. "And thumbs up if you found your book had different sections or chapters?" Thumbs went up. "Did anyone else find something that we can add to our chart about All-About books?"

Elicit from one child the observation that All-About books have headings.

Emily's hand shot up. "My book has titles on a lot of pages. Some pages even have a bunch."

"Can you show me what you mean?" I wanted to see the exact feature she was identifying. Emily pointed to bold headings in her book. "Oh! Yes. Emily's author has written with headings. Notice the little titles at the start of the sections in her book."

Emily nodded. "This page has one . . . two . . . titles." She progressed slowly down the page.

"Thumbs up if your book, like Emily's, has headings that name its different sections or chapters. The titles you find in the middle of pages are called *headings*. Authors write headings to tell readers the name of that section or that part. That way, readers know what they'll learn about in the next part."

"Let's follow Emily's advice and add headings to our list of what we notice in All-About books," I said, and added "Headings" to the chart.

Don't underestimate the power of the hand/finger metaphor in explaining the structure of All-About books.

This is the same active involvement we used two weeks ago when children were examining How-To books. It helps to be consistent as often as possible.

Notice this efficient way to gather and combine your children's observations. You may end up using this ritual often.

Often young children will not be able to read all the words that are on the pages. They can still notice features in these parts.

Obviously your children will probably notice something entirely different and so your minilesson will diverge from this one.

Be sure that children's ideas and words (as well as yours) get a place on the chart.

Have a child explain that All-About books often have a table of contents.

"Aiesha, will you explain what you told me you noticed about your book?"

"The first page is just like the first page in *Poppleton*, see, on this page it says 'Contents.' Then it has titles on one side and numbers on the other side. That's just like *Poppleton*."

I held up the copy of *Poppleton*. "So what you are saying is that when I read *Poppleton* aloud to the class, I told you that the first page was the contents page. And I showed you the list of chapter titles. Each title listed the page where it started." I put down *Poppleton* and picked up Aiesha's All-About book. "On this side are the titles of the different chapters, and on the other side are the page numbers."

Tell children how the table of contents helps the reader.

"The job of the table of contents is to tell the reader the titles of the sections or the chapters in the book. Let's now add a table of contents to our list as well," I said, writing it on the chart.

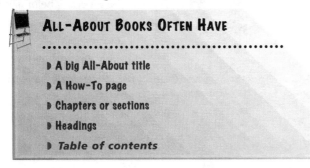

ALL-ABOUT BOOKS OFTEN HAVE

> A big All-About title
> A How-To page
> Chapters or sections
> Headings
> *Table of contents*

Link

Retell what your children have done and invite children to continue doing it.

"So far today we have looked over examples of the kind of writing we wanted to do. I know you will want to look more closely at All-About books. Keep the book I just passed out to you and continue to study it today. Today, let's spend most of writing workshop looking over All-About books."

Ask children to also make a list of possible topics.

"After you've studied what the pros do, get some paper from this tray and list possible topics you could write about."

You need to be sure your class has recently read a book with a table of contents that lists chapters. Draw attention to this structure when you read aloud. In this minilesson, when you send partnerships off to pore over books, join one partnership. Look at their book as if you are seeing it for the first time. Point out the table of contents: "Well, I'll be! Look at this. What do you suppose this is for?" Your children will quickly share your excitement. You will have set up the children to know that close study of texts pays off.

Although there are more features that can be found, don't try to list every one. Leave some to be discovered in the ensuing days. As your children continue to read more All-About books, they will discover new features of this genre and will love becoming famous for their discoveries.

You may be concerned at the idea of a class full of youngsters, each independently studying the features of nonfiction writing. Relax! Let the children approximate this as well as they can. It doesn't really matter that children notice any particular characteristics. It does matter that they have time to explore, to talk, to notice, and to rev themselves up for this new endeavor.

TIME TO CONFER

During today's writing workshop, children will look over published books, noticing decisions the authors of those books made. They may not be able to read the books, but they'll still be able to notice captions, labels, indexes, and the like. Instead of normal conferring, be prepared to gather clusters of children together and:

▶ Help these children see that a book has a big topic (aircraft) and then smaller topics (planes, spaceships, blimps) and that, in this example, the blimp page only contains blimp information and the plane page only has plane information. This can be an enthralling realization to a child.

▶ Help the children understand the system behind the page numbers that are listed alongside the chapter titles in the table of contents.

▶ Help children see that there are pictures that match the information in the words.

Once a few children have seen these things in one book, encourage them to look at more books so they come to understand these features are somewhat consistent across many of the books. See conference cited at right.

You'll also want to help children imagine possible topics they could write about. Help partnerships support each other in generating lists of possible topics.

This conference in *The Conferring Handbook* may be especially helpful today:

▶ *"What Will You Write in Your Table of Contents?"*

Also, if you have *Conferring with Primary Writers*, you may want to refer to the following conference:

▶ *"Where Is Your Author's Voice?"*

STRUCTURING ALL-ABOUT BOOKS: THE TABLE OF CONTENTS

GETTING READY

▶ List of topics you consider for your All-About book
▶ Table of contents paper
▶ "All-About Books Often Have" chart
▶ Cover paper
◉ See CD-ROM for resources

EARLIER I SUGGESTED THAT ONE *of the challenges children confront when they write non-narrative texts is that they can no longer rely on the sequence of time to structure their writing. It's easy, therefore, for them to end up with writing pieces that are "piles" of assorted stuff. So for this unit, we will use the table of contents as a way to teach children that writers divide topics into subtopics and then confine themselves to addressing one subtopic at a time.*

It is important to remember that children won't learn from what we do so much as from what they do. As teachers, then, we help enormously when we set up children so that they end up doing better work than they would have done without our scaffolding. Often the most efficient and effective time to intervene is early on, before children actually embark on pieces of writing.

When children write information texts in which they teach others what they know about a topic, the most important help we can give involves setting children up to write a lot about one and then another subtopic, addressing each subtopic on a separate page or in a separate section. This minilesson asks each child to anticipate the chapters he or she might write on a topic and to draft a table of contents. You will teach children to divide their topic into subtopics, to consider whether they have a few chunks of information related to each anticipated subtopic, and to address each subtopic on a separate sheet of paper.

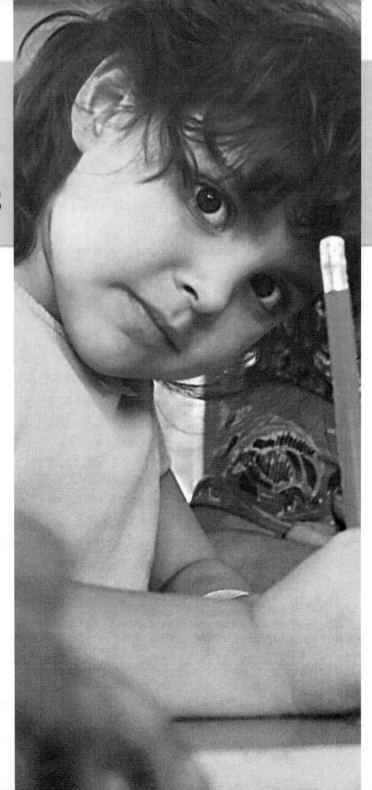

The Minilesson

Connection

Ask the children to let you know if they have an idea for a topic.

> "Thumbs up if you have an idea for what your topic will be for your All-About book. Great!"

Create an image of a bandleader at a concert. Have children announce their topic when called on.

> "Let's pretend this is a concert, and I am what you call the conductor. In a concert, the conductor stands at the front of all the instruments, at the front of the orchestra, and points to whichever instrument should play. So I'm going to conduct this orchestra. When I point to you, say your topic in a loud, clear voice. Okay. I'll give you a moment to get your topic in your mind. Do you have it? All right, here goes." Whenever I pointed to a child, the child announced his or her chosen topic.
>
> "Baseball."
>
> "Music."
>
> "The beach."
>
> "Snails."

Tell the children that today you will teach them how to "try on" their topics.

> "You have all chosen fascinating topics. I can tell I'm going to learn a lot! Today I am going to teach you how to 'try on' your topic so you know if your topic is a good topic for you."

Teach

Liken trying on a topic to trying on a sweater. Ask the children to watch as you "try on" several topics by imagining what you could say about each.

> "Writers 'try on' topics before we say, 'This is the one for me.' We try on topics just like we try on a sweater at the store before we buy it. Have you ever done that? Before I say, 'This is the one,' I sometimes put the sweater on, or I hold it up and think, 'Will this fit me? Will this work for me?' Writers do the same

This is one of many little rituals we use. Like the turn-and-talk ritual, this one can be put to many uses. Here it allows you to quickly overview the class while the children get a sense of what their classmates plan to choose as topics.

A child could conceivably select a topic such as "My Grandma" or "My Bedroom" and still write an All-About text. That is, the genre of non-narrative writing can be used for social studies and science topics such as clouds or the presidency but it is also possible to write a non-narrative text about topics of personal knowledge.

thing. I have a list of topics, and I'll show you how I try them on to see if they will work for me. You be researchers, watching what I do, so you learn how to try on a writing topic before you choose it. My list of possible topics goes like this:"

Possible Topics
- The flute
- Dogs
- Training a dog

"First I'll try on the topic of the flute." I gestured with my hands to show I was trying that topic on for size like I might try on a sweater. "I had a flute when I was little, but I didn't play it for long. Okay. I'm thinking, 'What do I know about the flute?' Umm, well—I remember it is an instrument and you blow into it and you push the keys and it sounds like a whistle, and . . . um . . . uh . . . well. That's sort of all I remember." I spoke with little energy, and then shrugged, making it very obvious that I neither knew nor cared about the topic.

"Let me try to think what my chapters would be if I wrote a book about the flute." By now the children had all forecast that this topic wouldn't work for me. "Chapter one could be what a flute looks like. It would be a short chapter, because I don't remember any details but I know it's shaped like a stick. Chapter two would be, um . . . be . . . um. Gosh, I'm realizing I'm not the best person to write about flutes. I tried on that topic and it didn't fit, so I'm crossing it out."

"Let me try on 'dogs.'" I hold the imaginary topic up against my torso. "That's easy. I could have these chapters:"

Dogs
- Kinds of dogs
- Dog shows (I watch them on TV)
- Feeding your dog (because I have two, so I know)
- Training your dog (I could write a whole book on that!)

I could now summarize the gist of the process of weighing different topics by saying, "After I listed these topics, I thought, 'Which would work for me?' and I realized I didn't know a lot about the flute and so I chose training a dog." But if my goal is to mentor children in the actions of mulling over and narrowing in on a topic, it is vastly more effective to reenact the process by "opening the top of my head" and saying aloud the thoughts as I have them. Notice that I think aloud in a step-by-step fashion, weighing one topic and then the next. I set up the children to beat me to my conclusions.

If I decide to use the metaphor of "trying on" and say that we try on a topic as we might try on a sweater, I'll repeat the same phrase often. I don't try to be creative by changing the words I use, alternating between trying on, testing, checking it out, previewing, and so on, or my minilesson will not have the coherence I want.

One could "try on" topics in lots of ways. I decide to do so by generating a list of subtopics because I'm steering the children to do this soon.

"So the topic of dogs fits me! Now let me try on the topic of 'training your dog' because I think I could write a whole book just about that one chapter. Let's see, I could write:"

Training Your Dog
- How to teach your dog to heel
- How to teach your dog to come when you call
- Different treats you could give your dog
- Questions and answers for what to do if your dog is hard to train
- Different books you can read to learn about training your dog

"So I have two topics that fit me, and I just need to decide which will make the better book."

Active Engagement

Find a child whose topic is familiar to all. Tell the class to identify some chapters that the child could possibly write on this topic.

"Earlier we heard that Christine might write about recess. Will you pretend that recess is on *your* list and practice trying on that topic? Work with your partner, and see if you can list across your fingers the chapters you might put in a book about recess. Think about whether you'd have a lot of interesting things to say in each of your chapters. See if this is one of the topics that *could* fit you." The room erupted with talk.

"I heard you guys say lots of things. You are right that in her book about recess, Christine could have a chapter on playing Red Rover and another chapter on walking up the slide. And she could have a chapter on different things you can do if it's a rainy-day recess."

Things to Do at Recess
- Playing Red Rover
- Walking *up* the slide
- Different kinds of things to do during a rainy-day recess

In Session X you'll show how you deliberate on the genre of each of your subtopics. It'll help if the first subtopic or two are How-To subtopics because your children will know a lot about that genre. It'll also help if a second or third subtopic addresses "different kinds of something" so that, after you remind children of what they know about the genre of How-To writing, you can teach this next genre. Don't select a subtopic that suggests a third genre unless your kids are strong writers and it is a clear and useful genre for which you have specially formatted paper. You won't use the "different kinds of something" paper or mention the genre implicit in any of these subtopics until Session X.

It's not an accident that Christine's topic is one the whole class can address—I wouldn't ask kids to imagine what they'd write about Christine's uncle!

Christine and her recess book won't be in your class. The topic you mention and the sub-topics will be incorporated into Session X's minilesson, so read ahead and overhear subtopics that will allow you to make the points you want to make. You can listen furiously, with extra intensity, or you can pretend (if you don't mind white lies). Say "I heard some of you suggest . . ." and then complete the sentence with whatever you wish you'd heard!

Link

Tell children that today they need to try on each of their topics and then start writing.

"So today, try on each of your topics. Talk about the different topic choices with your partner. If you have a topic that feels like it will work, then you can get a blank piece of table of contents paper," I held a piece up [Fig.VIII-1], "and start to write your table of contents."

"You don't have to finish the table of contents before you start writing chapter one. If you are ready to start writing, come and see me so I can help you decide on the paper you'll need. And remember, for the rest of your life, that before you write an All-About piece, it's good to try out your topic."

MID-WORKSHOP TEACHING POINT

Suggest to children as they work in their partnerships that one chapter can be How-To, like the books they have just written.

"Writers, I know you are listing different things you could write about that go with your topic. When you try to think of different chapters or sections, remember that *The Pumpkin Book* has a page for 'How to Carve a Pumpkin.' Maybe you can teach people how to do something with your topic. Maybe you can have a 'How to Play the Violin' chapter or a 'How to Stop When You Are Rollerskating' chapter, or a 'How to Do a Gymnastics Trick' chapter."

"And remember *The Pumpkin Book* also had a section on different kinds of pumpkins, like I had a section on different kinds of dogs and Christine had one on different kinds of things we do during indoor recess. Think about if you could have a chapter on different kinds of things that go with your topic."

Remind children to make covers for their books.

"Get back to work. After you list three or four topics, try to choose one. If you've made your choice, use cover paper and make yourself a cover."

Throughout these minilessons, we provide children with scaffolds. One is the table of contents paper, set up to remind children that they'll list chapters (their subtopics) and provide page numbers for each. Another scaffold is the frequent request to "list across your fingers." Yet another is the special paper they'll soon use within each chapter. Each page will be tailored to support the genre of that chapter.

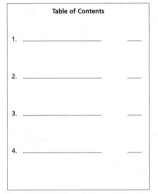

Fig. VIII-1 Table of Contents paper

Don't wait too long before you make this intervention.

The concept that a writer can elaborate on an idea by talking about the different parts or kinds of a topic is rich. Think, for example, about minilessons. What are the different kinds of minilessons? What are the different parts of this structure? How about the different kinds of conferences and the different parts of them?

TIME TO CONFER

It's early in your students' work with All-About writing, so your conferring will still be closely aligned to your minilessons. Your goals aren't particularly fancy:

▶ You want every child to have in mind a topic that you believe can sustain the child's interest for two weeks—one that the child knows something about. You may want to nudge your more experienced writers to select a focused topic. That is, a child could write a book on either a broad topic such as birds or a focused topic such as birds' feathers—the latter would be more challenging.

▶ A few children will have trouble imagining what might go in a table of contents. See "What Will You Write in Your Table of Contents?" from *The Conferring Handbook*.

▶ You want each child to begin imagining what he or she will write. Use a published book to provide the template and help a child who is writing about race cars realize that his topic will go on the cover, and then realize that the things he knows about race cars (kinds of them, famous drivers, what happens at a race) get listed on the Table of Contents page and that each topic on that list will then become a separate chapter.

▶ You may set up a few children for tomorrow's lesson by helping them see that some of their chapters are How-To chapters and will need How-To paper and others are different-kinds-of-things chapters and can profit from paper that supports this structure.

See the conference cited at right.

This conference in *The Conferring Handbook* may be especially helpful today:

▶ *"What Will You Write in Your Table of Contents?"*

Also, if you have *Conferring with Primary Writers*, you may want to refer to the following conference:

▶ "Where Is Your Author's Voice?"

AFTER-THE-WORKSHOP SHARE

Remind the children of their chart about the genre. Read each item from the chart while children point to where they've incorporated that item in their drafts.

"Yesterday I told you how my son Evan goes to the skate park and studies what kids who are practically pros do to pull off skateboard tricks. Then he comes home and tries the same things. And we studied Gail Gibbons, who is a pro at writing All-About books and we learned things she does to write All-About books." I revealed the chart the class had made the day before.

> ### ALL-ABOUT BOOKS OFTEN HAVE
> ....
> ▶ A big All-About title
> ▶ A How-To page
> ▶ Chapters or sections
> ▶ Headings
> ▶ Table of contents

"Many of us decided to try the same things. Let's check out what we've done and what we haven't done. Put your book (or your cover and your table of contents) in front of you. Okay. Let's reread our chart and check. All-About books often have 'a big All-About title.' If you have this, point to it. All-About books often have 'a How-To page.' If you have this, point to it. If you plan to have it, thumbs up. All-About books often have, 'chapters or sections.' Thumbs up if you plan to have those. And All-About books often have 'headings' and a 'table of contents.' If you have either of these, point to it."

Tell children that by reviewing charts, you often realize work you still need to do.

"Writers, when I reread charts and check my work, I sometimes realize things I need to do tomorrow. If rereading this chart gave you ideas for tomorrow, that's great."

There are a couple of wise moves in this share session. First, I very briefly review the trajectory of thought we've been on before moving forward into the new work of showing children how to use a chart to guide their review of their work and their plans for tomorrow. If we really do want today's work to stand on the shoulders of yesterday, it helps to show how today fits with what's gone before. This is something good readers do and good teachers do it as well. Then, too, it's important for us to think through the logistical challenges in our teaching so as to keep things as smooth as possible. First children lay yesterday's work out, then I reread one item from the chart, then each child points to where he or she incorporated this item in his or her writing, then I read the second item from the chart. The logistical forethought makes this doable.

Take home your students' writing right away and look at what they have done. Although they haven't written much at this point, you will get an early sense of whether their topic is taking them on the right journey. Your children's work will give you a window into their understanding of this new genre of nonfiction writing.

After you are fairly confident about your students' choice of topics, have a fast look at each child's table of contents. Because your children have recently studied the intricacies of How-To books and are probably quite adept at this kind of writing, you should expect to find How-To sections in every book. In fact, some of your students might choose to have even more than one. Nicole's table of contents lets us know that she is planning a section on how to feed a baby but also another one on how to change a baby's diaper. Melinda's All-About topic on cooking contains a "How to Make a Sandwich" section as well as a "How to Set the Table" section.

Then, too, you will expect to find that many children are planning a "different-kinds-of-something" section. Because your upcoming minilesson will include special paper for this kind of writing, decide whether you will work with some children to help them envision the possibilities within the topic. Carlos has planned a section on different kinds of toys. On the other hand, Felito has so far planned only a section on how to choose candy. Felito and children like him may need to see more examples of other possibilities and may need more individual conferences or small-group work. Why not plan now for how you will support these students over the next few days?

PLANNING EACH CHAPTER: CHOOSING PAPERS AND STRUCTURES

GETTING READY

- *The Pumpkin Book* and *Apples*, both by Gail Gibbons
- Supply of paper, including How-To paper and different-kinds-of-something paper
- Your own All-About book with a table of contents
- List of chapters related to the shared topic discussed in previous lessons
- See CD-ROM for resources

THIS SESSION MOVES WRITERS TO A DRAMATIC NEW LEVEL *of thinking. You'll suggest that when writers plan out their subtopics (or their chapters), they think not only, "What will I write on this page?" but also, "How will this chapter be organized?" Then writers select paper (and a genre) that matches their content. This, of course, is rich intellectual work even for you and me, let alone for five- and six-year-olds, but it is work that can be taught in such a simple, concrete fashion that we shouldn't be afraid to bring it to youngsters.*

Today, you'll show children that in some of their chapters they'll teach readers how to do something and will therefore want How-To paper (and will be using the How-To genre) and that in other chapters they will teach readers that there are different kinds of something and that these chapters will require paper that matches the design of their genre. (All forms of paper are on the CD-ROM.)

Connection

Tell the children that you'll teach them that when writing each chapter, the writer must select a genre and paper to match.

"Thumbs up if you have a topic for an All-About book. Great! Thumbs up if you tried out the topic by listing a bunch of different chapters you could write." Again, most children gave a thumbs up sign. "Great!"

"I know, too, that many of you looked at published All-About books to get ideas for your book. Today we'll look again at *The Pumpkin Book*, and I want to teach you that when we try to tell readers all about something, each of our chapters is like a new piece of writing. For each chapter, we need to think, 'What kind of paper do I need for this chapter?'"

Teach

Remind the children that when Gail Gibbons wrote her book she used particular features and a particular format.

"Remember when Gail Gibbons wrote a chapter on how to carve a pumpkin, she made this chapter into a How-To page and she titled it '*How to Carve a Pumpkin*' so readers would know what to expect. Then she used other helpers, too, to help us learn from her book. She wrote steps to take when carving a pumpkin and numbered them one, two, three, and so on. Remember how she had pictures to go with her words, pictures that taught people what to do? Here, in another book, *Apples*, Gibbons writes, 'How to Plant and Care for an Apple Tree,' and she does similar things."

Whenever possible, I make new points by referring to familiar rather than to new texts. It's easier for a child to focus on the new point (rather than on a new text as well) if everything but that one new point is kept consistent and familiar.

I am reminding children of what they learned earlier in this unit—and setting the stage for the lesson I'll teach today.

"In *your* All-About books, you (like Gail Gibbons) will probably have a How-To page or two. If you make a How-To page, use those same helpers!"

"Here in this bin, I've put paper that is set up so you can write a How-To page or two in your books. I know Marco will write how to build a castle, and Joline will write how to invent stories to go with the clouds. I know you guys will want to use this special how-to paper for those chapters."

Ask the children to tell their partner if they will write a How-To page inside their books, and if so, what will they teach people how to do.

"Tell your partner if you think you might use paper from this bin and write a How-To page within your book, and if so, what it will teach people how to do."

Show another chapter organized as a different genre, written on different paper.

"But often, instead of teaching us how to do something, Gail Gibbons wants to teach readers that there are a few—maybe three or four—kinds of something. Remember this page in *Apples*?" I showed the page "Some Common Apples Grown in North America." "Gail shows us there are different kinds of apples by cutting the page into parts, with each square showing a different kind of apple. And here, at the back of *Apples*, she has another page. This page tells different kinds of facts about apples. She again cuts the page into squares, and for each square she has a picture and a bunch of words telling more about the picture!"

Demonstrate rereading your table of contents, deciding on the genre and paper for each chapter.

"I realize that I need to reread my table of contents and decide what paper I need for each of my chapters. Watch how I decide, okay? Let's see . . ." I read from my earlier chart.

"Hmm, I guess that in this chapter I'd want to tell readers you need a leash and a collar, and I'd say that the first thing you do . . . Wait! That sounds like a How-To! I'll put the stuff you need up top like I put the stuff I needed to make cinnamon toast, then I tell the steps I take to train my dog to heel."

If I'm trying to make a general point, it usually helps to tell a few emblematic details—but only a few. When I say, "She used other helpers, too, to help us learn from her book," I follow this up by mentioning that she numbered her steps and provided pictures to match the words. But my goal in listing these details isn't to be comprehensive. It's to use these details as another way to make my general point. The same is true when I discuss what particular children will do. I don't cite more than two—Marco and Joline—because those two are enough to convey my general point.

Your purpose here is to show that each chapter needs to be ascribed a genre and given matching paper. To make this point, you need to move along quickly. No one kind of paper is crucial. You want your students to learn that non-narrative texts are structured in a variety of ways. Before a writer approaches a subtopic, he or she thinks, "How will I organize this?" The choices you demonstrate here are especially distinct and fundamental to non-narrative writing, but the fact that writers pause to consider their structure before writing a section is your most crucial point.

Again, each session revisits and builds on earlier sessions.

I reenact rather than summarize the process I go through to decide on the genre. Of course it's no accident that my first subtopic is written in the genre the class knows best.

I reread the next item on my list (as if to myself):

Then, as if I was just that moment becoming aware, said, "That's practically the same as 'teaching your dog to heel!'" I picked up another sheet of How-To paper. "I need How-To paper for that, too." Then I continued reading.

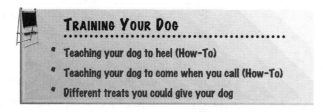

"Hmm, I'll say liver, bacon, dog biscuits . . . hmm, let's see. I'm thinking that I can't put step one, step two, if I want to tell about *the different treats* you can give your dog." As I spoke, I looked at the How-To paper, as if struggling to see how and if the content of a chapter on "Different Treats" could fit on the same paper (and in the same genre) as chapters on "Training Your Dog."

"I think this will need different-kinds-of-something paper!" I picked up a piece of paper that was sectioned into squares, each containing a box for a picture and lines for words. [*Fig. IX-1*]

Pointing to one of the four empty squares, I said, "I can write 'dog biscuit' here and draw a biscuit and tell about that. Then I can draw 'liver' and tell about that."

My hope is that by saying out loud a sequence of thoughts, I encourage children to think along the same path and they will beat me to the conclusion I end up reaching. I want them to conclude that if I'm telling about different kinds of treats for my dog, this "chapter" fits the different-kinds-of-something paper.

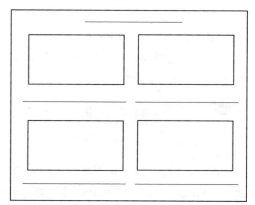

Fig. IX-1   Different-Kinds-of-Something paper

Active Engagement

Together, choose the genre for each chapter in the book the class planned in the preceding lesson. Ask the children to tell their partner the genre and paper they'd use for the first chapter.

"So if we, as a class, took Christine's idea and decided to write a book about recess," I referred to the list the class made previously of chapters Christine's book might contain, "do you think one of her chapters might be a how-to-do-something chapter written on paper like this?" I hold up a sheet of How-To paper. [*Fig IX-2*] I read aloud the list the class had made:

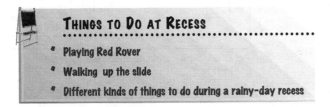

THINGS TO DO AT RECESS
....
* Playing Red Rover
* Walking up the slide
* Different kinds of things to do during a rainy-day recess

"Tell your partner if you see a chapter in Christine's recess book in which she could use How-To paper." Each child in the class turned to sit knee to knee with a partner, and soon everyone was talking.

Reconvene the class and say what you heard.

"I heard smart ideas. Christine *could* write, '*How to* Play Red Rover,' or '*How to* Walk Up the Slide' and she'd be smart to write those as How-To chapters. She'd have to think, 'What do we do first when we play that? Next? Next?' Some of you came up with more How-To chapters she hadn't even thought of yet. Christine could write '*How to* Jump Rope.' So she needs to get this kind of paper," I picked up a sheet from the bin full of How-To paper, "for those pages of her recess book."

I've carefully set up children for success. Obviously, the first two chapters on this list could be written as procedural text, which children have already learned how to do.

I worded the third item in this manner because otherwise each of these items could conceivably be written on How-To paper, which doesn't make my point.

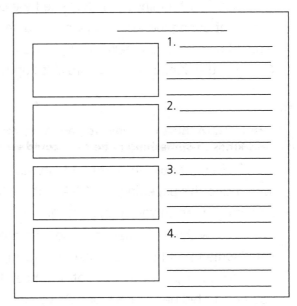

Fig. IX-2   How-To paper

Help children consider whether the same child's book might contain a chapter that requires different-kinds-of-something paper. (Be sure the answer is yes!)

"Now, listen up. Here is my next question. Do you suppose Christine could use *this* kind of paper and write about different kinds of something in her recess book?" I held up a piece of paper as shown in Figure IX-3.

Ask the children to imagine what they'd write in a chapter titled "Different Things We Do During Indoor Recess."

Pointing to the line at the top of the page where a title would go, I said, "You could write, 'Different Things We Do During Indoor Recess.' Hmm, what might go in these different boxes? Hmm, different things we do during indoor recess. Hmm. Will you think about what might go in the different sections of the paper? Tell your partner." The children began to talk excitedly.

After just a minute, I reconvened the class. "I heard you say we could write that during indoor recess we play games," I pointed to one square, "we read," I pointed to the next square, "and we talk. Or you could say, 'We play Clue, we play bingo, we play cards.' It's up to Christine."

Link

Ask the children to think of a How-To page they could write. Then ask them to think of a different-kinds-of-something page they could write.

"So right now, in your mind, do this. Think of a How-To page *you* could write using this paper in your All-About book." There was a long silence. "Thumbs up when you've thought of one.

"Now think of what could go on a different-kinds-of-something page *you* could write using this kind of paper." Again, there was a minute of silence. "Thumbs up if you've thought of this. Keep these pages in your mind now as you get started on today's work. As you leave the meeting, take whichever paper you'll need for your first bit of writing. If any of you are not sure how to get started, stay on the rug and we'll work together."

Fig. IX-3   Different-Kinds-of-Something paper

Again, I belabor these thoughts and let children come to conclusions before I do.

The sequence of our teaching is very important. The last words we say are those our children carry with them, so it's often wise to reiterate the main direction you want children to take.

The moment of silence is more important than you can imagine. Don't rush past it.

TIME TO CONFER

You'll find that a few children need you to walk them through the process of getting started on an All-About book. If you gather a cluster of these children for a strategy lesson, replicate the minilesson. That is, recruit the group to all help one child write and reread a list of chapters, then scan that list for, "Could any of these be a How-To chapter on this kind of paper?" With the children who need extra help, you'll want to go a step further and help the child write a starting sentence for his or her How-To chapter (just to establish the voice, point of view, and patterns of the text). Then set up this child to write about a chapter on the different kinds of a thing. Once the group has helped one child, set them up to help each other in partners while you watch and coach, intervening and then pulling back to let them continue without you. This should take six to eight minutes. See conferences cited at right.

After this, survey the room to see if others are well launched. Plan on convening another small group or two; there will be other kids who need help now, and strategy lessons will be more efficient than one-to-one conferences. See "What Will You Write in Your Table of Contents?" from *The Conferring Handbook*.

These conferences in *The Conferring Handbook* may be especially helpful today:

▶ "If There's No Punctuation, When I Read Your Report It Sounds Like Gobbledygook"

▶ "What Will You Write in Your Table of Contents?"

Also, if you have *Conferring with Primary Writers*, you may want to refer to the following conference:

▶ "Where Is Your Author's Voice?"

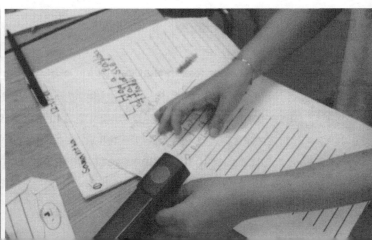

AFTER-THE-WORKSHOP SHARE

Tell the children about a writer who not only wrote a How-To page and a different-kinds-of-something page but who created another kind of page as well.

"Writers, I saw so many of you choosing paper wisely. Thumbs up if you made some decisions about the kinds of paper that you needed today. Great!"

"When Bethany and I were talking before, she noticed that in her table of contents, she had a page for how to do homework," I held up Bethany's How-To page, "and she had another page for all the different kinds of assignments that she does for homework." I held up the different-kinds-of-something paper. "But then Bethany did something really smart. Bethany, can you tell us what you put on this page today?"

"Well, you see," Bethany began, "I wanted to make a list of all the teachers. Like I wanted to write that Mrs. McGrath is the library teacher and Mr. Gonyea is the gym teacher. But I didn't have good paper for my list."

"So you got the idea to make your own paper!" I said, as if this was an unbelievably wise move on her part. "Show us how you solved your problem."

Bethany held up her list paper, which now contained a list of teachers' names. [*Fig. IX-4*]

Extrapolate a longer lesson that can guide other children.

"I hope some of you decide to include lists in your All-About books, or that some of you, like Bethany, invent new kinds of paper for chapters that have different structures. Will you tell your partner if you have a chapter that needs a kind of paper that we don't yet have in our writing center? Talk over whether you think you, like Bethany, will need to invent a kind of paper."

This quick reminder brings back into focus that today children learned to choose certain kinds of paper for their chapters. You want them to realize they need different kinds of paper because different chapters comprise different kinds of writing.

Bear in mind that in one-to-one conferences you can help a child do some new work, and then spotlight that work later (leaving off any mention of the role you played).

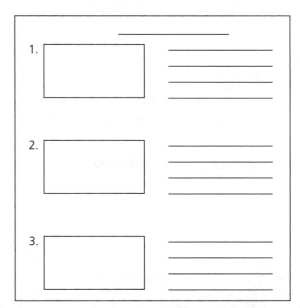

Fig. IX-4   List paper

Of course, we began this unit knowing that some chapters will contain lists and had planned all along to include list paper. Whenever possible, we want children to realize they can invent ideas. Our message is, "You, too, can think about your message and find a form, a genre, through which to convey your message."

This will have been a very important, provocative day in your writing workshop, and you'll definitely want to sit with your children's work and try to understand what they are thinking. Settle down for a long, rich look and expect to be astonished and intrigued by the meaning they do and do not seem to have made from the minilesson.

You'll probably find that it looks as if some children entirely missed the point. They may have been there in body but not in mind. Don't be discouraged. This is true in classes all over the world and has always been the case. After all, did we ever dream that the reason many third graders can't distinguish *to*, *too*, and *two* is that no one mentioned the different spellings? The interesting thing is to try to understand why some children seem to let the words of minilessons sail right past them. Can you alter their seating arrangement? Use their names more often in the course of a minilesson? Have a paraprofessional or a student teacher sit right beside them and elbow them, "Wow! Did you hear that!" during minilessons?

The lessons you tried to teach today were abstract. It's a lot to ask of a child to hear about structuring Christine's book and then extrapolate this point and transfer it to her own book. You'll just need to hold small-group strategy lessons with groups of children to reteach this. Don't hesitate to do this with them and even for them. They'll learn from writing in these forms even if you are the one to get them started.

Come to school with plans for the kids you need to reach right away. Call them together in groups of four. Remember, it's okay if you have to show a child that this one chapter can be a How-To chapter and this other one can be a different-kinds-of-something chapter. The children will learn from doing this work even if you have to carry them over the initial hard part.

MAKING LABELED DIAGRAMS

GETTING READY

▶ *The Pumpkin Book* by Gail Gibbons, some pages copied on transparencies
▶ Overhead projector
◉ See CD-ROM for resources

IN THE PREVIOUS LESSON *you taught children that each of the different chapters (or sections) in their All-About books will not only address a different topic but also be structured differently, with some chapters (or sections) as How-To writing and some divided into categories for different kinds of a thing.*

Today you'll reinforce the previous lesson and teach the children that writers can also teach readers about the different parts of a thing through labeled diagrams, some of which show particular parts close-up.

The Minilesson

Connection

Remind children that one of their chapters might be How-To writing, another might be a list or might describe different kinds of something.

"Yesterday we noticed that inside her book on pumpkins, Gail Gibbons had a chapter titled 'How to Carve a Pumpkin,' and she organized it the way we do with our How-To paper. She also had a 'Different Kinds of Pumpkins' page and organized it the way we do with our paper showing four different categories. Today I want to show you another kind of writing and another sort of paper writers can use."

Teach

Show children that Gibbons has a page that shows parts of some thing and suggest they could do the same.

"Let's look at Gibbons' *The Pumpkin Book*." Using the overhead projector, Laurie displayed a page from the book. "Notice that this page shows the *parts* of a pumpkin seed. As I notice what Gail Gibbons does, I'm getting ideas for what Lucy could do. I'm thinking in her How-To book on dogs, she might have a page that is titled, 'Parts of a Dog,' and she could label the chest, scruff, and things like that. And I think she could follow Gail's idea and draw and label a picture, so she'll want to use this kind of paper." She held it up. [*Fig. X-1*]

"I'm telling you this because you can do the exact same thing. You, too, could have a chapter on parts of a thing."

The secret to this unit is that you make differences in genre very concrete by relating each genre to a different format. You'll want to be able to show the children exemplar texts that contain different chapters or sections, each structured differently. Nonfiction texts almost always contain a patchwork of rhetorical structures but are often written in paragraphs that all appear, at a glance, to be similar. However, a closer look will show that one paragraph begins, "There are many reasons for . . . ," and another says, "Similar uprisings were happening in many places," or, "The process was always the same. Always, people would. . . ." For now you're relying on more graphic ways to convey rhetorical structures.

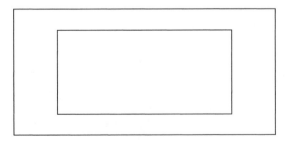

Fig. X-1   Parts of a Thing paper

Active Engagement

Ask the children to think of their topic and to imagine writing a 'Parts of a thing' chapter.

"Will each of you think of your topic, and tell your partner if you could imagine a chapter called, 'Parts of a [Blank]'? Think whether you could you have a page where you draw and label *your* topic? What might you write for your labels?" Children pulled close to their partners. Laurie listened in on two of them.

Nicole: "I think I want to make a page that has the parts of a baby. Then I can make a diagram of a baby, and I can write *eyes* and *ears* and *hand* and *foot*."

Cynthia: "Is it a girl baby or a boy baby?"

Nicole: "Umm [she obviously has not given this part much thought], I'm only going to put the parts in that *all* babies have."

Laurie reconvened the class. "I heard great ideas. Many of you will include a diagram of your subject, and you'll label the parts of a violin, or a beach, or a skateboard, or something else."

Link

Remind the children that when they plan their sub-topics (or chapters), they should think about the format and paper they'll need.

"So today, as you continue writing your All-About book, remember that whenever you start a new page, you need to think, 'Will I be teaching people how to do something?'" Laurie gestured toward a piece of How-To paper. "'Will I be teaching readers that there are different kinds of a thing?'" Laurie gestured toward the different-kinds-of-something paper. "'Will I be teaching that there are different *parts* of something?'" Laurie gestured toward the page on which the parts of a pumpkin seed were labeled. "You'll need to choose the paper that matches your chapter."

It's ambitious to think that children can organize and write an All-About book in which each chapter contains a different rhetorical structure. Our saving grace is that each of these structures will be easily within the grasp of most of your children.

The gestures help a lot, especially your English language learners.

TIME TO CONFER

By now you hope your children approach their writing thinking of both their subtopic and the form or genre in which they will write, deliberately selecting paper to match their intentions. You can even post yourself beside the paper supplies, conferring with writers as they decide between kinds of paper, asking each to tell you about the writing he will be doing next. Does he tell you about genre and subtopic? You might ask him to touch sections of the paper saying what he is planning to write.

Some children won't be able to do this. A child writing a book on basketball might say, "Um, I'll tell about the ball an' stuff." Encourage her to muse over the questions, "What will the whole chapter be about?" and "What kind of thing will I write?" If she has difficulty, help her. "The ball. . . . Will that be part of a chapter on the different kinds of equipment for playing basketball? Will you use 'different kinds' of paper and draw the different things people need?"

When children tell what they plan to write, you can match that content to a genre you've already introduced. "So were you thinking this chapter would be a Small Moment story (or a How-To chapter, or a diagram with labeled parts, etc.)?" Sometimes, children will need help inventing a new genre. Teach children new ways to organize their writing: questions and answers, summaries, interviews, musings. You might say, "Yours is a *new* way to write. We should explain it to everyone and make a new kind of paper!"

Your students will now be immersed in their writing. The levels of support that you provide will vary. A few children will still need to flesh out the parts of their book. Many will need assistance with paper choice.

These conferences in *The Conferring Handbook* may be especially helpful today:

- ▶ *"Make a Mental Movie of Yourself Following Your Directions to Test Them for Clarity"*
- ▶ *"What Will You Write in Your Table of Contents?"*
- ▶ *"If There's No Punctuation, When I Read Your Report It Sounds Like Gobbledygook"*

Also, if you have *Conferring with Primary Writers*, you may want to refer to the conferences in part six.

Ask children to search with you in published books for other organizational structures to use in All-About books.

"Today we talked about making a parts-of page in your All-About books. You can get ideas for other pages and for the special paper they require by looking at published All-About books. Let's try it together, okay? Will one of you come up and look through this book and find a page where you think Gail has done something we could learn from?"

Rosa settled on the last page in Gibbons' book, which was a catalog of facts about pumpkins.

Suggest children can try these structures in their own books.

"How interesting. What a great choice! This is a different page. Gail Gibbons made a page full of interesting facts that she knew her reader would want to know. Decide with your partner if you can include a similar page in your book."

By now, you should anticipate that instruction is usually sequenced so that in the end, we invite and support initiative, invention, and independence.

MAKING TEXTS THAT TEACH

GETTING READY

▶ All-About books in which the children have been writing (ask them to sit on them until it is time to attend to them)

○ See CD-ROM for resources

TEACHING CHILDREN TO WRITE *is like teaching them to swim. There is very little you can do from the front of the class to make your children good swimmers. If they are going to learn these strokes, they need to do them. Therefore, you wisely describe a technique for a minute or two and then get into the pool. "Come on in," you say, and get them to try what you have described. "That's it. I love the way you are. . . ." And then you notice one thing they need to do differently. "The only thing I'd suggest is. . . ."*

By this time in your study of All-About writing, you will have spent plenty of time on the side of the pool, describing the moves you want your children to make. Now they need to plunge in, and you need to watch, and to be ready to say, "That's it. The only thing I'd suggest is. . . ."

The challenge is to think, "When I watch my children doing this, what can I imagine teaching that might make a difference?" In this session, you will respond to your children's tendency to share feelings rather than teach facts. You'll respond to the fact that they seem more apt to write, "I love cats. They are cute and nice," rather than, "Persian cats have long fluffy hair."

In this session, you remind the children that All-About books contain information and ideas, and you encourage them to become students of their subject, gathering bits of information they can include in their books.

THE MINILESSON

Connection

Remind children they are trying to teach about the subject of their books.

"For the last few weeks, you have been writing books that teach. Last night I took your All-About books home and studied them. I realized that I want to talk to you today about being teachers because that is what you are when you write teaching books."

"In my town, there are classes for grown-ups. I can sign up to go to a cooking class or a computer class or a flower class. I recently took a class on flowers."

"I sat in the chair with all these other grown-ups in the other chairs." I acted out my words, demonstrating that I sat diligently, an eager student. "I was ready for our class on flowers. Our teacher came in and he looked at us. He said, 'Today I will teach you about flowers.' Then he said," (and my intonation suggested this would hardly be adequate instruction) "'Flowers are nice. Flowers are pretty. I love flowers. Flowers are great, great, great. Some flowers are red, some flowers are yellow. All flowers are pretty.' Then he said, 'Class is over. You can go home.'"

Looking out at the children, I asked, "Do you think that was a very good class?"

In unison, the children chorused, "No!"

"You're right. I said to that teacher, 'But, but, but . . . I didn't learn anything yet.' You see, when a teacher says, 'Come to my class on flowers,' the teacher is sort of making a promise. The teacher is promising to teach people about flowers."

Explain that when a writer writes a teaching book, the writer is teaching a class on the subject.

"Writers, I am telling you this because when you write an All-About book,

I suspect children listen much more attentively because I tell this as a story.

This is not the usual connection. I haven't gone back and summarized what I have taught over the last few days, showing how today's session adds on to those prior lessons. Instead, I contextualize today's lesson in a broader way by reminding children that at the start of this unit I said they'd graduated and were now ready to be teachers as well as writers. And I let them know I want to talk more about what it means to be a teacher. Then I try to help them understand the problem I saw in much of their writing by regaling them with an exaggerated story of a teacher who tries to teach by merely giving platitudes. My hope is that some of them will realize that they sometimes do this too.

you are the teacher. And when you give people your book," I gestured to show a child handing someone his or her book, "you are saying, 'Come take my class on flowers'—or cats—or recess—or stickers. And *you* are sort of making a promise. You are promising to teach people about your topic."

"If I come to your class, if I read your book, and it just says, 'Cats are cute, cats are nice, cats are sweet, I love cats,' and I don't learn anything, then when I finish reading your book, when it says 'The end, you can go home now,' I'm going to say, 'But, but, but . . . I didn't learn anything yet.'"

"Whenever you write a teaching book, you need to make sure you don't break your promise. You have to teach your reader. Today I will show you how to do that."

Teach

Tell the children to ask, "What do I have to teach that my reader might not already know." Demonstrate.

"Teaching is sort of like giving, and if I am going to teach you about my topic, I have to think, 'What do I have that I can give you?' So if I were going to teach people about our recess time, I'd have to think, 'What do I have to give them—to teach them—about recess?'"

"Watch me getting ready to teach grown-ups about our recess because pretty soon I am going to ask each of you to teach people about your topic."

"So first I think, 'What do I know about our recess?' Hmm. I know kids play at recess, but I bet *everyone* knows that! Hmm. What do I know about recess that grown-ups might not know? Maybe I could teach them about the special games you all play at our recess—like yesterday, I saw you all making a long train on the slide, with each of you holding someone's waist. I bet they don't know about that! And I bet they don't know that you play King of the Castle on the pile of tires! I could say which games lots of kids play and which games some kids play."

Remind children to ask, "What do I know that I could teach?" and tell them writers of All-About books must ask this.

"Did you notice that when I wanted to write a teaching book on recess, I

This minilesson folds back on itself. I tell the story of a teacher who doesn't deliver in a way that we expect and therefore lets us down, and then I suggest that my students, like that teacher, need to actually teach or else they, like the teacher, will let people down. Because I am trying to suggest that my students are similar to that teacher, I use the same terms to describe the teacher as I use to describe my students.

The teaching method I use in this minilesson is demonstration. Therefore I reenact step by step the procedure I go through as a writer. Because I want my children to learn from this demonstration, the subject that I choose to write about in my role-play is a topic on which each of my children is an authority. This way, my role-playing is more apt to be within their reach. Also, the topic—recess—is the same one I wove through my earlier minilessons. I don't want to jump around in a chaotic fashion, role-playing one day that I am writing about cats and another day about recess. By keeping many aspects of my minilesson simple and consistent, I spotlight the teaching point I am trying to make.

asked myself, 'What do I know that I could teach people?' and even, 'What do I know that they might not know?' Those are questions writers who are teachers need to ask."

Active Engagement

Ask the children to reread yesterday's writing counting how many things they taught readers.

"In a minute, I am going to ask you to open your book to the page or two you wrote yesterday. Then I am going to ask you to read what you wrote yesterday and, on your fingers, count up how many *new things* you taught your readers during yesterday's writing. Do that now. Let's each work alone, quietly."

Asking children to do something on their own, quietly, while they sit before you on the rug is much more powerful than you might think. Be sure you don't break the spell by talking with a child during this interval. If you have been writing your own All-About book along with the children, tell them, "I'll do this too," and model the activity. Otherwise say, "I'm going to admire you as you work," but don't ever talk one-on-one or they'll get restless.

Set up children to practice teaching about yesterday's topic with a partner.

"Writers, can I have your eyes up here please?" I waited for their attention. "Will you think of your topic? Think, 'What do I know about that topic that I *could* teach people?' Squeeze your mind. Think, 'I could teach them that . . .' and see if you come up with something you know that your reader might not know. Do that quietly."

Speak as if your words can mobilize every child to do this—and they can! Give them time; expect their minds to be doing as you suggest.

"So partner one. Right now, you are the teacher. And partner two has come to take a course with you on your topic. Say to your partner, 'Hello. Today I am going to teach you about . . .'—you say the topic. Then teach your partner some things you know. Okay. So partner one, start off by saying, 'I am going to teach. . . .' Begin."

As the children talked, I moved among them, encouraging the teaching partner to give examples and to provide details and encouraging the listening partner to ask questions.

This is an important part of this lesson. You are positioning your children to adopt the mindframe that is fundamental to this kind of writing. The goal of this lesson is to convey to children that when they write information texts, they need to teach others about their topic; that is, it isn't enough for them simply to comment on or talk about their topics. Instead, they need to think of something to teach and then teach it. Here, you set up kids to do this, much as a person does who runs along behind a bicycle, getting a novice bicycler up and going.

Remind students of what they are doing well and ask partners to switch roles.

"Teachers, I loved the way many of you told your students little tiny details about baseball and Frisbees and baby brothers. You didn't just say 'You can play games,' you told particular games! You didn't just say, "Baby brothers are messy,' you told particular ways that they are messy.

"Will partner two now become the teacher? Start off by saying, 'I am going to teach you about. . . .' And don't forget to be detailed. Give examples."

Link

Remind the children that when they write teaching books, they are promising to teach.

"Writers, remember that whenever you write a teaching book, you make a promise to your reader. Your reader comes to your book like I came to that man's course on flowers. Your reader wants to learn stuff, just like I wanted to learn at that class. And when the teacher just goes, 'Flowers are nice, flowers are great, I like flowers,' I said, 'No fair. You promised to teach me.' Remember, when you write a teaching book, you are making a promise that you will teach us."

MID-WORKSHOP TEACHING POINT

If children are searching for something to teach readers, they can think of information pertaining to their topics and numbers.

"Writers, some of you are having trouble thinking of all the stuff you know on your topic. Let me show you something. Right now, think of your topic." I waited. "So I am thinking of recess. One thing you can teach people is, you can teach them *numbers* that go with a topic. So I am thinking about the numbers that go with recess. Umm. Well, the number of minutes is twenty minutes, recess is twenty minutes long. The number of swings we have is eight. The number of kids that can get on one swing at a time is two. So I could put those numbers in a teaching book about recess. Will you and your partner see if you can come up with numbers about *your* topic?"

Here I tuck a follow-up point under the main message of the minilesson. I expect that the stronger writers may pick up on this pointer and that it will fly over the heads of others.

Notice that once again my link circles back to earlier aspects of the minilesson.

It is crucial that we not only assign but also teach. It would have been easy simply to exhort children to make their books informative. The challenge instead is to equip them to do this. It's a little challenging to come up with guidelines like these because it's not really clear what will equip kids for the mental actions that are so fundamental to writing well. In this instance, I thought, "What do I do when I am trying to drum up something to say?" and I invented this suggestion. You will come up with others to share. Some will pan out; some won't. The point is, we need to do more than simply tell kids what we hope they will do.

Remind children they can teach their readers names related to their topics.

"Writers, another thing you can teach people is the names of things. Like I could teach them the names of our playground aides—Ms. Merriman and Mr. Flax—and I could teach them the names of the games you guys play, like Red Rover and Spud. Tell your partner names of things that go with your topic." Again, the children began to talk excitedly.

"I heard Maggie telling her partner the names of parts of the violin, and Sherry said the names of different kinds of pizza."

Remind children they can share advice or weird facts related to their topics.

"Writers, another thing you can do to teach people is to share advice. I could tell readers, 'At recess, don't forget your coat or you'll have to go back and get it.' Will you tell your partner advice you could give your reader on your topic?"

"One of the most fun things to put in your book is something weird about your topic. I learned yesterday that each mosquito has one hundred fifty teeth. I can't put that in my recess book, but if you know something really weird and interesting about your topic, tell it to your partner and definitely put it in your book." Again, the room was filled with talk.

"I heard Keisha say that pigs only have four toes on each foot! That is definitely something Keisha should include in her book!"

I learned about the number of a mosquito's teeth from the lid of a Snapple drink. As teachers, we collect whatever we can and weave it together into instruction.

TIME TO CONFER

This minilesson posed some interesting challenges for your students. There will be children returning to their text who are trying to see if their teaching book is really teaching. You can also expect to have many conferences with your students showing them various types of information that they might want to incorporate into their text. Many of these conferences can also be done with small groups of children as strategy lessons. Because you encouraged your students to look at books, it will be helpful to have a few carefully selected books on hand to refer to in your conferences. Here are some tips to remember. These tips are listed in more detail on the CD.

- Help a child weave advice into the rest of the book. Show her the option of a "Remember to" section (*Click*) or "Helpful Hints."
- Help a childe find a "home" for a weird fact. Show him how to make a new section, "Can You Believe This" or "Fun Facts." (*Click, Recycle*)
- Help a child see different ways to use numbers in relation to his topic (weight, year, kinds of, length of time).
- Help a child see different ways to use names in relation to her topic (lists of places, related people).
- If a child has written factual information, help her to reread her writing and find a place that she might want to add her own thoughts or response.

These conferences in *The Conferring Handbook* may be especially helpful today:

- *"Make a Mental Movie of Yourself Following Your Directions to Test Them for Clarity"*
- *"What Will You Write in Your Table of Contents?"*
- *"If There's No Punctuation, When I Read Your Report It Sounds Like Gobbledygook"*

Also, if you have *Conferring with Primary Writers*, you may want to refer to the conferences in part six.

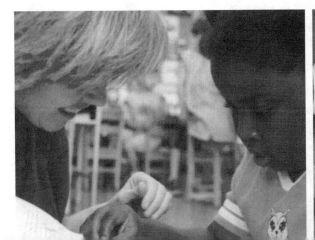

AFTER-THE WORKSHOP SHARE

Tell the children that some of them realized they needed to learn more before they could teach others. Send them off in small groups to study realated nonfiction books, to inform their texts.

"Writers, some of you aren't sure you really know enough about your topic to write a teaching book that really teaches. And that's a very smart thing to realize. But I want to tell you a secret. The way teachers get smart is, we study our topics. There are books written on most of your topics. I don't have books on everybody's topics, but I do have many. And I thought you guys could read these books together, and work together to see if the books can teach you things that you can add to your books."

"If you learn things that you want to put in your book, you know how to revise to add information, don't you?

"So, right now, will Emily and Melinda come up? I have a book for you two. And will Napoleon and Michael come up? I have a book for you the two of you as well." Soon the class was full of children reading books related to the topics on which they were writing.

Encourage writers to bring these "study books" into the reading workshop and to take them home that evening, continuing to read them.

After five minutes, I intervened. "Writers, may I stop you? Writing time is over, but many of you have asked whether you can bring these books into the reading workshop and whether you can take them home in your book baggies tonight, and the answer to both questions is yes. It is a great idea to get really smart on the topic about which you are writing."

If you are worried about children copying from these books and want to caution them to put what they learn into their own words, you can do so. With these children, it didn't seem necessary. This wasn't an issue for us yet.

It's wise to encourage children to take these books home because their caregivers can help them to read them.

Suggest that students observe the world to learn about their topic, not just read about it.

"Writers, I know that many of you will be taking home books on your topic to learn more information, but I want to tell you that another way that writers study their topic is to use their eyes to see what they can learn. So today, I can imagine that Napoleon can study the fire engines when he passes the firehouse on the way home. And I can imagine that Micali might stop and look at all the flowers she passes on the way home. This is called observation, and today, see if there is something that you can observe that will make you smarter about your topic. Make sure you take some paper so that, as you are doing this important work, you can draw pictures and write words about what you are seeing, and then tomorrow you can add the new information to your writing."

This added tip makes your teaching point a more inclusive one.

- Today's mid-workshop advice or share or minilesson can easily become a minilesson for a second or third day. If you decide to do that, for today's share have two children teach the class about their subjects.

- You could help the children know that it is important to think, "What might my reader want to know more about?" and even to anticipate the particular questions a reader might ask, adding information that will answer these questions. One of the guiding principles of this kind of writing is, "Answer your readers' questions when they ask them."

- You could suggest that the children prepare for this kind of writing by using the prompt, "I will teach you that. . . ."

- You could ask the children to reread their writing looking for sections that can be deleted. When I do this with my own writing, I speak of these as sections of my text that don't earn their keep. That metaphor won't work for children, but you can find a way to convey that sometimes they've chatted on and on about a topic and their words are sort of empty. What a great thing it is for writers to realize "I wasn't really saying anything there" and to delete those passages.

- You may want to encourage the children to listen to writing done by one another, by you, or by other authors, noticing when and how writers put information into their text.

- If your children are old enough, you might notice together the kinds of information writers include in their texts: numbers, quotations, definitions, history, warnings, instructions, and so on.

ASSESSMENT

You will definitely want to see what this minilesson yielded. If you simply collect children's work and take it home, you won't know which sections of children's writing were written today and which already existed. You may therefore want to take a moment at the end of today's writing workshop to ask children to mark where today's writing work began. Then you can look over at least a sampling of their pieces to see whether today's minilesson helped the children include more information. If you don't see much of an effect, you will probably want to revisit this concept for another day or two.

Rigor comes from pursuing a line of thought or work. Once you see children including more information, you can say to yourself either "Good, that's done," or "So that's done. What's next?" Every step forward opens up new horizons. If children are including information, you can extend this in a host of ways. For example, you will probably find that children throw facts together without a lot of thought about the order of these facts. You can also show them that not only do writers include facts and other tidbits of information, they also reflect on these facts. It'd be great if children learned the rhythm of writing with a fact, then of surrounding that fact with some thoughts and commentary.

REVISING: LEARNING FROM EACH OTHER'S WRITING

GETTING READY

▶ Pre-selected book, by a writer in the class, that contains a feature or features that can be emulated by other children

● See CD-ROM for resources

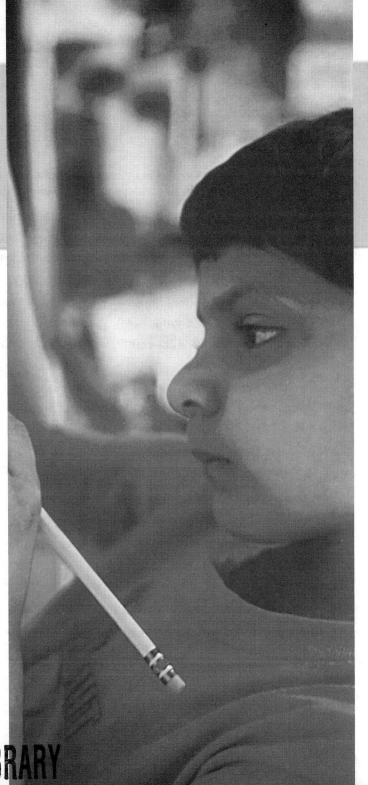

YOU HAVE NOW INVESTED *several weeks in your study of nonfiction writing. It is time to round the bend toward publication. Revision will be a bit different in this unit because your children have not written the usual stack of texts from which they select their favorite to fix and fancy up. Instead, they have written one multifaceted All-About book. You'll need to decide whether you want them to publish only a few revised pages from the book or to publish the entire book with only a few pages reread and reconsidered.*

We decided that it was important for our writers to produce very long books on their subjects and that we would be satisfied if the children each revised a few pages. We arranged for parents to come in and staff a publishing center so that the children's final books could be typed and eventually circulated as part of the school's library.

In this session, you remind children that one way to fix up a text is to study what other authors have done, emulating aspects of the authors' work. The surprise is that the authors you encourage your children to study and emulate will be their classmates.

THE MINILESSON

Connection

Tell the children that the world is dying to read their books, and name the publication date when their books will become part of the school library.

"Writers, I took your work home last night and your books were so great! I started reading bits of them aloud to my husband. He was repairing a broken machine and I said, 'Listen to this,' and I read a bit of Jose's book. Then I started to walk away and he said, 'Laurie, read on. Don't stop.'"

"The same thing happens when I read aloud to you, right? You say to me, 'Don't stop!' That is what my husband said to me last night. 'Don't stop reading.' Finally he said, 'Laurie, when will those books be in the library? I need to check them out.'"

"That got me thinking. I think the books you have written need to go not just in the class library but in the school library. So before school this morning, I asked Mrs. McKenzie if she had a shelf where they could go, and you should have seen how excited she got. While I was still talking to her, she started cleaning off this huge shelf."

"So, I know you would like to keep on working on your books, but I think your readers can't wait much longer! Folks are dying to read what you have written. How about if we send letters home today to see if any moms or dads or caretakers could come in and set up a publishing center, and how about if we try to get these books published next Friday? That means that starting this second, we need to fix up and fancy up our books."

Remind writers that they know how to fix and fancy up their books. Tell them that one way to improve writing is to emulate a famous author, and suggest they join you in doing this now.

"You already know lots of ways to fix up your books. I want to remind you that one of the smartest things a writer can do is to say, 'Let me study what another author has done and see if that gives me ideas for how to make my

We know that when we tell our children an anecdote about something that happened in our lives, the kids listen with rapt attention. When we set out to make a few points, we are less assured of their attention. Therefore, it makes sense to spin our points into stories when we can.

Laurie is letting children know in advance that publishing day is coming up and that their books will be circulated in the school library. We tap an energy source when we plan the details of publication, and it makes sense to engineer things so this energy can fuel our children's revisions.

You will set children up with the idea that they will be studying a famous writer and then surprise them by having this be a classmate. In his book On Writing Well, *William Zinsser suggests that surprise is one of the most important qualities of good writing, and it is a quality of good teaching as well.*

work even better.' You remember how we studied books by Gail Gibbons and Angela Johnson and Donald Crews. So I wanted to remind you that writers study books by famous writers, noticing what those writers have done. Then writers sometimes say, 'I can do that!' Today, let's all study a famous writer together right now, and then during the workshop you can study other famous authors."

Teach

Tell the children that the previous night you read a nonfiction book, paused to say wow about the writing, and went back to study what the author had done as a writer. In this instance, the famous author was a classmate, Rachel, who had written some facts and responses to those facts.

"Last night, I was reading a nonfiction book and after a page or two, I stopped and said to myself, 'Wow. This is nicely written.' So then I did what I usually do when I really admire the way something is written. I went back and reread it and thought, 'What did the writer do that worked so well?'"

Ask the class to look at the passage with you.

"Let's do that together. I want to read you just a part of this famous author's book, and I know that you, like me, will say, 'Wow, that was nicely written.' So listen. The book is called *All About Butterflies*, and it is by a writer named Rachel." The class giggled at that because Rachel was one of them! [*Fig. XII-1*]

Offer children copies of the text to study, and demonstrate how you study it.

"I know you are probably saying just what I said. 'Wow, that is really well written!' I figured you'd want to do what I do when I really love what an author has done, so I typed up these pages from Rachel's book. I am going to reread what Rachel wrote and show you how I study well-written writing. Remember when we saw that Angela Johnson had a comeback phrase and we tried to do the same thing? Well, we need to think, 'What has Rachel done?' so we can do the same thing! Watch me study her writing. 'Some butterflies do not have antennae. That is very strange. Why would some butterflies not have antennae?'"

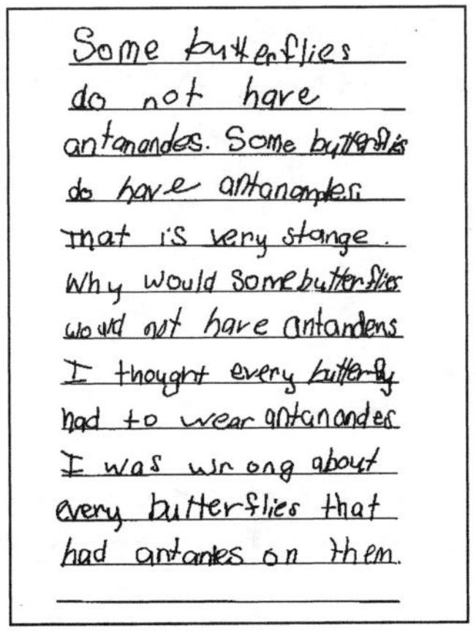

Some butterflies do not have antanandes. Some butterflies do have antanandes. That is very stange. Why would some butterflies would not have antandens I thought every butterfly had to wear antanandes I was wrong about every butterflies that had antanes on them.

Some butterflies do not have antennae. Some butterflies do have antennae. That is very strange. Why would some butterflies not have antennae. I thought every butterfly had to wear antennae. I was wrong about every butterfly that had antennae on them.

Fig. XII-1 Rachel

Show children how you look back on what you've read and reflect on why it works. In this instance, Laurie notices that Rachel has written down information and then written her thoughts about that information.

"I am noticing that Rachel wrote a really interesting fact about butterflies, and then she *thought about* the fact and she put her thoughts right here. See— she wrote 'Some butterflies do not have antennae.' And then she thought about that: 'Wow. That is really weird. I thought all butterflies had to wear antennae.' Then she wrote a second fact. [*Fig. XII-2*] Rachel added her thoughts to her book! I love the way she writes with information and then she wraps the information up in her thoughts about it!"

Laurie turned to the children. "Do you see how I reread just a little of Rachel's book, and then I stopped and asked myself, 'So what did Rachel do to make this good? What do I notice?'"

Active Engagement

Set children up to do as you have just done. Read the next bit of writing aloud, and ask partners to discuss what works about the way it is written. Collect one or two children's thoughts.

"Let's continue rereading Rachel's book and stopping to ask, 'What has she done to make this so good?' This time I will read a bit aloud and then when I stop, will you and your partner do the thinking work that we always do when we study an author? Ask yourselves, 'What has she done to make this so good?' Ask, 'What do we notice this writer doing that we could maybe do?' Okay, listen: 'When you touch the butterfly's wing, the scale will come off. I felt very sad. . . . If I was a butterfly, and someone would touch the wing, I would be very sad. . . . I would never touch a butterfly's wing. . . .'"

When children write All-About books, they often pile in a great many undigested bits of information. It should be a priority to teach children to pull back from the information to reflect on it. Children's reflections often will not be analytical . . . but the act of commentting on information is important.

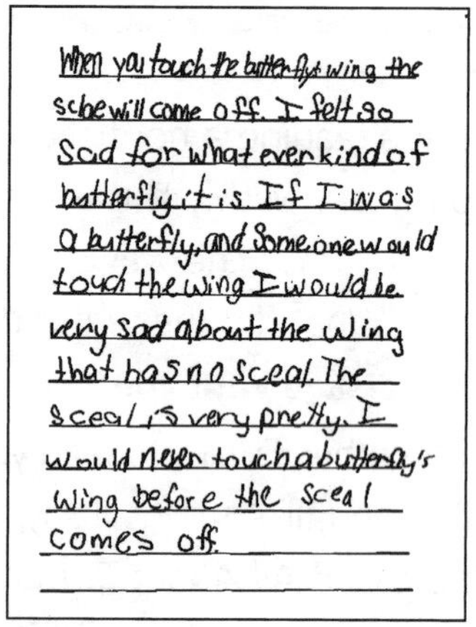

When you touch the butterfly's wing, the scale will come off. I felt so sad for whatever kind of butterfly it is. If I was a butterfly, and someone would touch the wing, I would be very sad about the wing that has no scale. The scale is very pretty, I would never touch a butterfly's wing before the scale comes off.

Fig. XII-1 Rachel

Laurie has set it up so the second page from Rachel's book illustrates the same point. The supposed point of her minilesson—that authors emulate work they admire—is only half of the message. She also wants to emphasize the particular lesson she is learning from Rachel's work. For this reason, both her examples elaborate on this single quality of good writing.

"Turn and talk to your partner." As children talked briefly with each other, Laurie listened in on their conversations. Mario burst out, "She does it again! She writes with facts, and then puts her thoughts about those facts."

After a minute, Laurie intervened. "Writers, many of you noticed Rachel doing the exact same thing. She again told a fact about the scale coming off when you touch a butterfly's wing, and again she thought about that fact and added her thoughts."

Tell the children that writers try to bring what they learn from other writers into their own writing. Recruit children to reread a page from a child's All-About book and to help her revise this page based on what you've learned together. In this case, you are revising to add responses to information.

"The next thing we do when we learn from writers is we think, 'So could I do the same thing?' I have asked Christine to reread a page from her book about recess, and would you all think if there is a way she could revise her book so that she does the same as Rachel. Here is one page of her book. Christine will reread it and then would you and your partner think whether she could bring Rachel's technique of writing with facts *and ideas* into her writing?"

Christine read, "'The monkey bars are very high up and very long. There are fifteen rungs. Some kids can't get across it and they fall down in the sand. The sand is not soft and fluffy, it is like rock.'"

"Turn and talk." Again, Laurie listened to the conversations, which predictably suggested that yes, indeed, Christine could add her response to her information.

"So, can anyone show Christine a way she could bring Rachel's technique of writing with facts *and* thoughts into her writing?" Soon Christine added a sentence responding to the information about the hard-as-rock sand under the monkey bars.

Whether you choose to select a child to read her piece of writing or whether your read your own writing is not important. What is important is that the topic is one that is familiar to your students.

Notice that we give Rachel ownership of the notion that writers write with information and ideas! It's wise to give ideas social currency.

This could be a very long minilesson. Don't let it be! Each of these turn-and-talks can be less than a minute long! You could also decide to bypass some of them.

Link

Remind children that some of them will include not only facts but also their thoughts about the facts. Others will emulate other authors and learn other strategies.

"Writers, you need to work really hard fixing up your writing today. I know some of you will want to reread your writing like Christine reread her recess book and make sure you wrote not only with information but also with your thoughts about that information. If you don't have room on the page to add your thoughts about information, use paper strips. (I have put some at each of your tables.) Some of you will want to study the work of other authors—and they could be authors from this class! Still others of you will want to make sure that you are doing a lot of teaching in your books, and that you have brought in information you learned from reading and from having smart thoughts about your subject."

"If you know what you are going to do first today, thumbs up. Okay, off you go. If any of you want some extra help getting started, bring your books and join me on the rug."

MID-WORKSHOP TEACHING POINT

Interrupt the children to show them how one child in the class tried out something she learned from another class author.

"Writers, can I stop all of you? I want to show you some of the smart things I saw in the class today. Maggie decided that she wanted to study another famous author, so she asked Jhumpa, 'May I read your book?" And then Maggie noticed that Jhumpa had question pages, where she asked a question and then answered it. Jhumpa asked, 'What do you need to go horseback riding?' and then she told about everything you need to go horseback riding. Maggie tried the same thing, only she asked a question that goes with her book. She wrote a question and then she answered it." See Figure XII-3.

It's not a bad idea to whip up a chart of ways writers fix up their teaching books. But the minilesson has gone on long enough that you'll probably want to disperse the kids. Perhaps one way to review what you have just said is to recruit a small group to help you make the chart. Then you can show the class how to use such a chart to guide their practice.

Why Does Dessert
Taste Good?
Fruit Salad
Strawberry Shortcake.
Dessert tastes good
because it is sweet.
Fudge is sweet and so is
donut and chocolate
cake.

Fig. XII-3   Maggie

Some of your children will fare well with the combination of options you've given them and, with the prospect of an imminent publication date, they'll set to work with great gusto. But there will be others who probably find it hard to know where to start.

You may want to respond by convening a group of kids who are taking a while to settle down to any one endeavor. Ask these kids to turn to the page of their book that holds the most information and then to reread that page with the intention of adding more of their thoughts about that information.

You'd help a lot by walking these children through the logistics of this work. Suggest that what you do when you want to revise to add more of your own thoughts to a text is that first you reread and put stars wherever you think you could add in some of your thoughts. Then give them paper, cut into five-inch-wide swatches. "Where you've put a star, this will tell readers to come over to this paper to read what comes next," you can say. "Over here, write your ideas and your thoughts about your information. Then you can tape it right on. Remember to keep learning from all the smart writers in this class."

These conferences in *The Conferring Handbook* may be especially helpful today:

- *"Make a Mental Movie of Yourself Following Your Directions to Test Them for Clarity"*
- *"What Will You Write in Your Table of Contents?"*
- *"If There's No Punctuation, When I Read Your Report It Sounds Like Gobbledygook"*

Also, if you have *Conferring with Primary Writers*, you may want to refer to the conferences in part six.

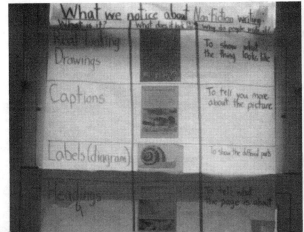

AFTER-THE-WORKSHOP SHARE

Gather the class together to revise the All-About Books Chart.

"Let's go back to our chart and add the new things we have learned that we might find in All-About books. I'm going to read what we have written so far." Laurie read the chart that had previously been created.

Ask the children to talk to their partners about what else they see often in All-About books. Listen in on their conversations and take notes on what children are saying.

"What else can we often find in All-About books? Turn and talk to your partner about other things that you might find in All-About books, and I'll come around and listen in." As Laurie moved among children, she jotted down notes.

Add the observations to the list in a few words.

"I heard so many smart things. I just had to write them down so I can add them to our chart."

Laurie added a few more features to the existing chart, and before long the chart looked like the one in Figure XII-4.

Tell the children that you will make this chart available as a check-off sheet. Compare it with the same one they used when they were studying How-To writing.

"Writers, I'm going to turn this chart into a check-off sheet, and you can use it as a guide for revision, just like you did when we were writing How-To books. Over here are all the things that we often find in All-About books." Laurie pointed to the far left list on the paper. "As you reread your book, put a check under the 'Yes' column if it is something you have in your book, and if not, put a check under the 'Not Yet' column. Then you will need to decide if it is a feature that you want to add to your All-About book. I'll put the check-off sheet in your writing folder for tomorrow's writing workshop."

If charts are to be used well, they need to be current so children can rely on them as resources. The charts provide a vehicle for accumulating instruction across days.

Laurie takes notes for two reasons. She wants to emphasize that even though children are talking with each other, not reporting to the entire class, what they have to say is still important. Second, she wants to be able to report the new features they have mentioned.

You'll make a copy of this chart for each child. If your children can't read the chart, you'll want to read it aloud once they have copies and to give them time to see whether their All-About book has each feature, marking their charts appropriately.

ALL-ABOUT BOOKS OFTEN HAVE

- A big All-About title
- A How-To page
- Chapters or sections
- Headings
- Table of contents
- A different-kinds-of-something page
- A parts-of page
- A fun-facts page

Fig. XII-4

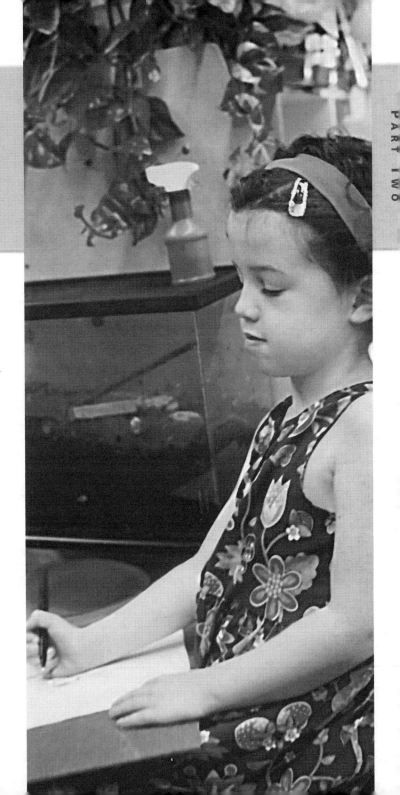

REVISING: FITTING INFORMATION INTO WRITING

GETTING READY

▶ Pre-selected writing by a child in the class that contains information that will need to be deleted or moved to another part of the book

● See CD-ROM for resources

YOUR TEACHING GROWS OUT OF WHAT YOU SEE *your children needing and out of your goals for this unit. During the early sessions, you emphasized that before writers of All-About books can begin writing, they need to divide their subject into subcategories, perhaps by laying out a table of contents containing chapters, each of which addresses a different aspect of the overall topic. It is no small accomplishment for five-, six-, and seven-year-old children to learn that writers don't just put everything that is in any way related to a topic into a chaotic heap but that instead they try to sort and control their information. You want to be very sure that your children have learned to categorize their information and ideas so that the material is at least organized by subtopic. (Ideally, your most experienced writers may have learned that a chapter about dog food can also have subcategories, with information about dog breakfasts grouped into one section of the chapter and information about dog dinners grouped into another section.)*

As you move toward your celebration of your children's All-About books, you will want to revisit the fundamental idea that nonfiction writers categorize their information by subtopic. You will encourage writers to reread what they have written, checking to make sure that the information in each chapter fits under the chapter heading. You'll help writers learn that extraneous information needs to be either deleted or moved to a more appropriate place.

Connection

Review the ways in which the children are revising and tell them you will teach one new way: to check that their writing is organized.

"Yesterday you guys did some really important work fixing up your writing. You learned from other authors and especially from Rachel, who wrote with facts and her thoughts about those facts. You made sure your teaching book actually taught. You used a check sheet to see if you'd done all the things that All-About writers do."

"Today I want to remind you of one last way that All-About writers fix up their writing. I want to teach you that writers check to make sure their writing is organized, to make sure it is sorted out right."

Teach

Ask whether the children have ever encountered a drawer that was intended for one thing but contained a whole mess of extraneous items. Suggest that writing can sometimes be that way.

"Have you ever opened up a drawer—maybe a kitchen drawer, where you are supposed to keep pot holders and dish towels—and then you realize that by mistake the drawer contains wires and tools and a hairbrush? Well, sometimes when we read over our writing, we'll find that a chapter that is supposed to be about one thing has a whole lot of extra junk in it."

This is probably not a good day to introduce something very ambitious. Your minilesson today will be straightforward and it will not require a lot of follow-up.

Laurie doesn't just say, "I will teach you one more way to fix up your writing." She names the way. There is no reason to keep children guessing about what you will teach; putting this information into the connection is a reminder that telling children to do something can't be equated with teaching them to do it.

Tell the children that one of their classmates wants to know if she has extraneous bits, so you have suggested that she reread her writing to the whole class. Together the class will help her clear out extra information.

"Writers, Christine is trying to decide whether all her information is in the right section, so I have suggested that we can all help. I've asked Christine to choose one chapter in her book and to read it aloud slowly and to tell us what she is thinking."

Christine began to read. [*Fig. XIII-1*]

Interrupt the student author after the first sentence and teach her to ask, "Does my sentence fit the chapter?"

"Christine, can I stop you now? Can you check to see if all your information fits your chapter? Ask yourself the question, 'Does all my information go in the chapter 'Games We Play at Recess'?" Christine nods yes and reads on.

"'Kids play with bouncing balls, like Four Square.'"

Laurie interrupted again. "Does that go in the chapter 'Games We Play at Recess'?"

"Yes, this goes here," Christine said and read more. "I like to play Four Square with my cousins and one time at their house in Ohio they had a tournament . . ." Suddenly she stopped. "When I asked, 'Does this go in the chapter on Games We Play at Recess?' I said, 'No!'"

"Good for you, Christine. You asked yourself the question and you knew the answer was 'no.' Can I show you what I do when I have information that doesn't belong? I make a giant cross-out, like this." Laurie demonstrated on another paper what a cross-out looked like. Christine took her paper and made the same symbol.

"Can I read more?" Christine asked. "'Our playground is very nice. It was made a lot of years ago by the parents of the fifth graders. . . .'"

Laurie chooses Christine because Christine is a fairly confident student, writing on a topic the class knows well, and because Laurie knows Christine's text contains information which needs rearranging.

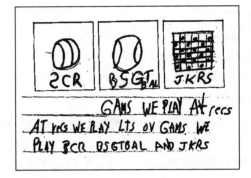

Fig. XIII-1   Christine

Games We Play at Recess. At recess, we play lots of games. We play soccer basketball and checkers.

Christine has realized that her chapter contains some extraneous information that needs to be deleted or moved elsewhere. When Laurie says, "Can I show you what I do when I have information that doesn't belong?" she elevates the situation and shows Christine that even grown-up writers encounter these problems.

Active Engagement

Ask the children to pretend they are the student author, rereading the next bit of writing and asking, "Does this sentence fit under the subtopic of the chapter?"

"Tell your partner what you think Christine is asking herself and what she will answer."

Children turned to talk in pairs, and they quickly agreed that Christine had again asked, "Does this go in a chapter 'Games We Play at Recess'?" and that the assessment was no.

"What did you think?" Laurie asked. "Christine, since this is your book, do you want to answer it?"

"I asked, 'Does this go in Games on the Playground?' and I said no, so it is in the garbage."

"Do the rest of you agree or disagree with Christine?"

"We agree because how the playground got built isn't a game, it is for real."

"I thought the same thing. I thought, 'Wait a minute! This is about the history of the playground, not the games we play.' But, Christine, you don't have to put it in the garbage. This part about the history seems so important, so look." Laurie showed the children how Christine could scissor that part out and create a new chapter for it.

Link

Ask the children to get started doing this on the rug. Send them off once they are well begun.

"Today, writers, will you get out your books right now, and while you are on the rug, will you start rereading them? Remember, first reread the chapter title. Then reread what is under the title, asking, 'Does this go here?' You will have to cross things out like I did, and to move things too. This work will be really important for you to do for the rest of your life, whenever you write in chapters or in categories. Get started, and when I see you well on your way, I'll send you quietly off to your writing nooks."

This is a very tidy form of active involvement. I think of it as a teacher doing something in front of children, then passing the baton on to them and saying, "Keep going."

In a minilesson we teach a single point. But as this minilesson illustrates, we can make other little pointers along the way, enriching our instruction.

Often your minilessons suggest optional strategies that a writer might try that day or another day soon. This minilesson obviously is different. You want to be sure that every writer has some time to check for structure, and consequently you get everyone started doing so while they are still on the rug, under your thumb.

TIME TO CONFER

Today, you will probably want to have one-to-one conferences with some children whose writing raises fundamental issues. Perhaps the night before when you reread your children's work, you noticed that a few children's writing often doesn't make sense. You'll want to be sure to help these children reread for sense, expecting to revise. Try also to ascertain the cause of the problem. Is the issue that these children write so slowly that their syntax is compromised? Is the issue that this child is so worried about misspellings that he avoids challenging words? Is the problem that the child rushes, leaving gaps that she doesn't see because she is always moving forward, never rereading? Remember that each struggler struggles in his or her own way, and you give a child a great gift if you can get to the root of the problem.

In conferences with strugglers, the research component is extra important, and it will often involve you saying, "So do that now while I watch." These children will not (and need not) be good at articulating their mental processes. You will need to be the one to see what's going on in their minds. Take the time to do this. You can get that time if you keep in mind it does children no good whatsoever for you to walk though their entire texts telling them why they did a million different things wrong. Teach one thing that your research suggests might really help. Teach that one thing today, tomorrow, and again next week.

These conferences in *The Conferring Handbook* may be especially helpful today:

- "*Make a Mental Movie of Yourself Following Your Directions to Test Them for Clarity*"
- "*What Will You Write in Your Table of Contents?*"
- "*If There's No Punctuation, When I Read Your Report It Sounds Like Gobbledygook*"

Also, if you have *Conferring with Primary Writers*, you may want to refer to the conferences in part six.

Tell the class some examples of students who are checking to see if their information fits where they've put it.

"Writers, I want to share with you the smart things I have seen you all doing today as you reread your writing and checked for order. Brittany was rereading her book, *All About Beaches*, and she came to chapter one, "Water." She thought, 'I will check to see if all this goes in a chapter on water.' So she reread her piece. [*Fig. XIII-2*] 'When you go to the water you can see waves. And watch some people swim in the water.' 'Yup, that fits,' Brittany thought."

"Then she reread some more: 'There are waves in the water.' 'Yup, all of that has to do with water,' she thought to herself. Then she came to the next chapter, chapter two, Sand. And she reread that page to herself: 'You can make a sand castle because it uses up the sand.' 'Yup, that fits in this chapter.'"

"'You can find many kinds of shells in the sand. Some shells look like a potato chip with ridges.' Then she thought, 'Wait a minute. Does this go with sand?' No—and then she did a smart thing. Look. Now she moved that information to the chapter on shells where it belongs."

"Damien is writing a book all about cars. Damien did the same thing as Brittany; he reread his chapter on the parts of the car to see if his words fit." He read Figure XIII-3. "'The steering wheel helps you to drive. The mirror helps you to see. The gas pedal helps you drive. If you speed, you will get a speeding ticket.' 'Uh-oh,' he said. 'This doesn't fit.' And he put a circle around it because he knew he needed to make a new section."

Remind students that they can be doing the same thing.

"I hope some others of you are finding ways to make your information fit into your story just right!"

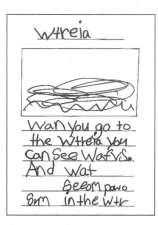

When you go to the water you can see waves. And watch some people swim in the water.

Fig. XIII-2   Brittany

The steering wheel helps you to drive. The mirror helps you to see. The gas pedal helps you drive. If you speed, you will get a speeding ticket.

Fig. XIII-3   Damien

EDITING: BECOMING RESOURCEFUL WORD SOLVERS

GETTING READY

- Whiteboards
- Dry-erase board, markers
- Index card for new word wall word
- See CD-ROM for resources

AS THIS INFORMATIONAL STUDY ENDS, *it is important to remind children that before they publish their work, they need to reread it, attending to conventions. Children at this time in the year are familiar with checking the word wall. In your previous study of How-To books, you taught them to check the word wall for commonly used words. In this minilesson, you will teach children how to be resourceful word solvers as they face bigger words.*

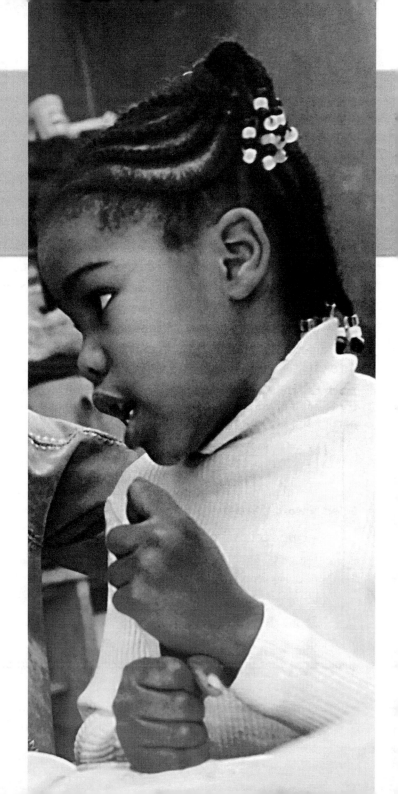

THE MINILESSON

Connection

Congratulate the children for working so hard and tell them they need to get their books ready to be published.

"Yesterday, many of you revised your pieces of writing, and today we are going to get our writing ready for publication. Many of you have been using some really big words, like *ingredients* and *directions*, or other big words, like Maggie used *fingerboard* and Melinda used *restaurant*. First, I want to congratulate you for being brave and trying those big new words, and today I want to teach you how you can be word solvers."

Teach

Teach the children that when you are a word solver, you try out various strategies to try to spell a word and that one way to do this is by looking for little words that are a part of the big word.

"Sometimes, when I want to use a word that is really big and I don't know how to spell it, I ask myself, 'Is there a little word in the big word that I do know?' Let me show you."

Select a word that many children have used in their writing.

"Let's choose the word *about*. So first, I say the word aloud." Laurie said the word again. "*About.* Then I ask myself a question: 'Is there any little word in that big word that I know?'" Laurie thought for a few seconds. "*Out.* I know the word *out.*" Laurie said the word slowly and then wrote it quickly: "*O-u-t.* Okay. So if I know out, now I am going to try to write *about.*" Laurie slowly stretches out the word, then writes *a-b-o-u-t.* "Everybody try to write the word *about*, since it is in all your titles. Remember, think of the little word *out* that is part of *about.* I'm going to add *about* to our word wall." Laurie gets out the index card that the children know will soon find its way to the word wall "How should I spell *about*?"

The class responded, in unison, "A, b, o, u, t."

I love using words like bravery *and* courage *to describe young spellers. They are apt words!*

Notice that Laurie is using the teaching method of demonstrating. She is re-enacting her processes in front of children rather than simply summarizing them. Almost three-quarters of these minilessons revolve around demonstrations, so it is worth noticing the details of this method.

Call on one child to try to be a word solver with a big word. Lead the child through the entire process.

     "I've asked Melinda if she will be a word solver. Melinda was really brave and tried to write the word *violin*. I've asked her to try to spell *violin* again on our board now that she knows something that she can do when she comes to a big word."

     Melinda's eyes moved alternately between the dry-erase board and her book. Then she started to laugh. "I spelled *violin [viln]* wrong. I can't even *squeeze* in the letters. I asked myself the question about little words, and I know the word *in*. I forget to put in the *i*." Melinda wrote *vilin*.

Notice the continuity. Here, again, spellers are described as brave.

Active Engagement

Tell the children to tell their partner things that the word solver did.

     "Will you turn and talk to your partner and tell your partner everything you saw Melinda doing? Make believe you are writing a How-To page, How to Check the Words in the Title of Your All-About Book."

     Napoleon: "First Melinda got her book. Next she found the word on the page."

     Christine: "Then she asked herself a question. 'Is there a little word?'"

     Napoleon: "Then she laughed because she didn't write the word *in*."

     Christine: "So then she wrote *in*. *Violin*."

Be sure the class learns a lesson about editing that can be used in other ways.

     "So now you know that when you are writing a big word, look for little words that might be in the big word."

Because the order of the checking process is important, Laurie refers back to the recent How-To study and asks children to think in the air.

Link

Ask the children to remember to make sure that the words that are in the title are also spelled correctly if they use them on other pages of their book.

     "So, today when you go back to your seats, you will be getting your books ready for publishing. Be brave and look at those big words. And be sure you check the new word wall words throughout your book."

When you confer with children about conventions, remember that when you first look at what a child has done, it can look "all wrong." But usually something that is wrong is only partly wrong; if you look more closely, you'll see the child's work is also partly right. Your first job is to find and name for the child the part that is partly right. Often the "partly-right" parts were accidental. If you support these successes, you can make them deliberate next time.

Then you can address the part that is partly wrong. For example, a child uses periods when she pauses. That's partly smart work on her part, but the resulting text now has fragments. You'll want to show her that she needs to reread each sentence and ask, "Does this make sense? Did I cut this sentence into too-small bits?"

Errors are windows to the child's mind. Don't brush them aside without trying to find the theories that guide this child. Can you discern the logic behind the error? If not, ask the child to explain why she did this or that. Listen with an open mind, trying to fully comprehend (not yet to fix) her theories. Then when you talk back, you can show her ways her theory will and won't work. See conference cited at right.

The conferences in *The Conferring Handbook* may be especially helpful today:

▶ *"If There's No Punctuation, When I Read Your Report It Sounds Like Gobbledydook"*

▶ *"Famous Writers Use Periods to Tell Readers When to Stop"*

Also, if you have *Conferring with Primary Writers*, you may want to refer to the conferences in part six.

After-the-Workshop Share

Set up a way for children to read each other's work and talk about it.

This is the final day for this part of the nonfiction study. Today you will want to celebrate all the writing that the children have done. You may want to arrange the tables for a "museum" share and give children the opportunity to read one another's books. Set the tone by telling them that today they will have the opportunity to learn so much that they never knew before. Allow extra time because the children will be moving around the room and looking at other students' work.

You will have been studying your children's writing with an eye toward organization, structure, information, and clarity. Tonight, you may want to look at your children's work with an eye toward growth in spelling and punctuation. Many of your children will be progressing well in this dimension of their writing, but there will be others who continue to cause you (and their parents) concern. Take their writing home, and set their nonfiction writing alongside work they have done throughout the year. Try to notice patterns of growth and areas of ongoing need. Here are some questions you can ask:

▸ What seems to come easily for this writer? Which words or chunks of words does the writer appear to "just know"? You will have taught your children many words by now that they can spell in a snap. When this child writes some of those high frequency words incorrectly, does it seem to you that the writer tried to rely on a visual memory of those words and just got them wrong, or is this writer caught in a rut of trying to sound out too many words? In general, sounding out words won't work as an efficient spelling strategy past December of first grade because after that, too many of the words a child wants to read and write will be irregular.

▸ Does this child seem to have well-developed phonological awareness? Does the child seem to hear and represent each sound heard in a word (even if he or she represents them inaccurately)? Does the child seem to hear the difference between *our* and *are*? Can the child hear that the initial sound in *initial is* not the same as in *engine*? If the child seems to have some difficulty hearing and differentiating sounds (as opposed to matching those sounds to correct letters), then you (or the speech teacher in your school, who is usually well trained in this) may want to give the child a little extra help in phonological awareness.

▶ Does the child seem to have an effective strategy for breaking long, hard words down into constituent parts, saying a part of the word and writing that part down, then rereading what's on the page to locate the word chunk that comes next, then recording that chunk, and again rereading what is now on the page?

▶ Is the child relying on what he or she knows when tackling unfamiliar words? One of the most useful strategies is spelling by analogy. If a child keeps his or her nose to the ground, tackling each word left to right, letter by letter, that child will be an inefficient and inaccurate speller. You need to help this child ask, "What do I know that can help me with this word (or this part of a word)?" and then rely on that knowledge.

CELEBRATING NONFICTION WRITING: CEREMONIAL BOOK PLACEMENT

GETTING READY

▶ Bookshelf that has been cleared and will house the new books. Make a sign to place over the shelf that says "All-About Books"

▶ Mortarboard-type hat for each child

▶ Flower made out of tissue paper for each child

▶ Paper titled "What Information Did You Learn From Your Book?"

▶ Prior to today, time for students to practice reading their book

▶ Prior to today, a letter to parents and caregivers letting them know of the accomplishments and of the upcoming celebration

▶ Light refreshments to be served at the end of the celebration

▶ Portion of "Pomp and Circumstance" you used at the beginning of this unit, to play, sing, or hum

● See CD-ROM for resources

AT THE START OF THIS UNIT, *you promised your children that they would be not only writers but teachers. When you celebrated How-To books, you had children teach small seminars to clusters of classmates and parents. You could, of course, decide to do a variation of that again as part of the celebration of your children's All-About books. This time, you might have your children go to another class—perhaps a kindergarten classroom if they are first graders—to teach others about their subjects. But the most important thing you can do is to see that your children's books are housed in the school library alongside other nonfiction books. You will probably set aside a special shelf for these books; alternatively, you could create a number of subject-based displays, intermingling some of your children's books with a small collection of published books on the same topic. Obviously, anything you do involving the school library will take some prior arrangements—and will also require that your children's books have been corrected, word-processed, and illustrated. Print out several copies of each book so that one set can be in circulation in your class library, another can be sent home with proud parents, and a final set can be displayed in the school library.*

You will want to prepare for this celebration. With your children, practice the ceremony described next. Have your children make decorations to dress up the library's bookshelf and their books, both. Remember, as Byrd Baylor tells us, "You are in charge of the celebration!"

THE CELEBRATION

Arrange the children with their books and an audience for them. Greet everyone and open the ceremony.

Our class of children and their parents and caretakers had gathered in the school library. The adults sat on chairs arranged near a large bookshelf, the sort that displays books so that their covers can be seen. The children clustered on the floor in front of the adults, each child holding the book she or he had written.

"Welcome guests and welcome writers, today is a very big day! Your writing will not only be published, it will be put in the school library so the whole world can read your books and learn from you. You really and truly have graduated to a whole new level! So today, we're going to have a graduation ceremony. Writers, can you take your places?"

Ask children to line up with graduation hats. Play or hum music, and invite the children in to put their books in the library. Offer them a flower or other token as you and others congratulate them.

The children headed to the hall with me, where I lined them up and gave each a mortarboard. Each child was still carrying his or her book, and the books each had a decorated cover. Back in the library, Laurie began playing an audiotape of "Pomp and Circumstance." The first child solemnly paraded through the door of the library, along the path we'd cleared. She carried her book in her hands, as if she were a ring bearer at a wedding, and walked with regal poise. At the bookshelf, the writer turned and set her book on the shelf. Then she approached Laurie, who said, "Congratulations, Author," and gave her a flower. The proud writer continued parading en route to the library's exit door as the next writer approached the bookshelf.

After the ceremony, give writers time to talk over their books and learning as they snack with the guests.

Once the books had all been arranged in their proper place, it was time for celebratory drinks and food and some small-group conversations in which children told one another and the grown-ups what they learned.